MAURICE BLANCHOT

Without Maurice Blanchot literary theory as we know it today would be unthinkable. Jacques Derrida, Paul de Man, Michel Foucault, Roland Barthes, Gilles Deleuze: all are key theorists crucially influenced by Blanchot's work.

This accessible guide:

*   works 'idea by idea' through Blanchot's writings, anchoring them in historical and intellectual contexts
*   examines Blanchot's understanding of literature, death, ethics and politics and the relationship between these themes
*   unravels even Blanchot's most complex ideas for the beginner
*   sketches the lasting impact of Blanchot's work on the field of critical theory

For those trying to get to grips with contemporary literary theory and modern French thought, the best advice is to start at the beginning: begin with Blanchot, and begin with this guide.

Ullrich Haase lectures at Manchester Metropolitan University, and **William Large** at the College of St Mark and St John, Plymouth.

Routledge Critical Thinkers:
essential guides for literary studies

Series editor: Robert Eaglestone, Royal Holloway, University of London

Routledge Critical Thinkers is a series of accessible introductions to key figures in contemporary critical thought.

With a unique focus on historical and intellectual contexts, each volume examines a key theorist's:

- significance
- motivation
- key ideas and their sources
- impact on other thinkers

Concluding with extensively annotated guides to further reading, *Routledge Critical Thinkers* are the literature student's passport to today's most exciting critical thought.

Already available:
Fredric Jameson by Adam Roberts
Jean Baudrillard by Richard J. Lane
Paul de Man by Martin McQuillan
Edward Said by Bill Ashcroft and Pal Ahluwalia
Maurice Blanchot by Ullrich Haase and William Large
Sigmund Freud by Pamela Thurschwell

For further details on this series, see *www.literature.routledge.com/rct*

MAURICE BLANCHOT

Ullrich Haase and William Large

London and New York

First published 2001
by Routledge
2 Park Square, Milton Park, Abingdon, Oxon, OX14 4RN

Simultaneously published in the USA and Canada
by Routledge
270 Madison Ave, New York NY 10016

Routledge is an imprint of the Taylor & Francis Group

Transferred to Digital Printing 2005

Typeset in Perpetua by Taylor & Francis Books Ltd

British Library Cataloguing in Publication Data
A catalogue record for this book is available from the British Library

Library of Congress Cataloging in Publication Data
Haase, Ullrich M., 1962–
Maurice Blanchot/Ullrich Haase and William Large.
Includes bibliographical references and index.
1. Blanchot, Maurice–Philosophy. I. Large, William, 1963– II. Title.

PQ2603.L3343 Z673 2001
843'.912–dc21   00-062808

ISBN 0–415–23495–6 (hbk)
ISBN 0–415–23496–4 (pbk)

Printed and bound by Antony Rowe Ltd, Eastbourne

CONTENTS

SERIES EDITOR'S PREFACE

The books in this series offer introductions to major critical thinkers who have influenced literary studies and the humanities. The *Routledge Critical Thinkers* series provides the books you can turn to first when a new name or concept appears in your studies.

Each book will equip you to approach a key thinker's original texts by explaining her or his key ideas, putting them into context and, perhaps most importantly, showing you why this thinker is considered to be significant. The emphasis is on concise, clearly written guides which do not presuppose a specialist knowledge. Although the focus is on particular figures, the series stresses that no critical thinker ever existed in a vacuum but, instead, emerged from a broader intellectual, cultural and social history. Finally, these books will act as a bridge between you and the thinker's original texts: not replacing them but rather complementing what she or he wrote.

These books are necessary for a number of reasons. In his 1997 autobiography, *Not Entitled*, the literary critic Frank Kermode wrote of a time in the 1960s:

> On beautiful summer lawns, young people lay together all night, recovering from their daytime exertions and listening to a troupe of Balinese musicians. Under their blankets or their sleeping bags, they would chat drowsily about the gurus of the time ... What they repeated was largely hearsay; hence my lunchtime suggestion, quite impromptu, for a series of short, very cheap books offering authoritative but intelligible introductions to such figures.

There is still a need for 'authoritative and intelligible introductions'.

But this series reflects a different world from the 1960s. New thinkers have emerged and the reputations of others have risen and fallen, as new research has developed. New methodologies and challenging ideas have spread through the arts and humanities. The study of literature is no longer – if it ever was – simply the study and evaluation of poems, novels and plays. It is also the study of the ideas, issues and difficulties which arise in any literary text and in its interpretation. Other arts and humanities subjects have changed in analogous ways.

With these changes, new problems have emerged. The ideas and issues behind these radical changes in the humanities are often presented without reference to wider contexts or as theories which you can simply 'add on' to the texts you read. Certainly, there's nothing wrong with picking out selected ideas or using what comes to hand – indeed, some thinkers have argued that this is, in fact, all we can do. However, it is sometimes forgotten that each new idea comes from the pattern and development of somebody's thought and it is important to study the range and context of their ideas. Against theories 'floating in space', the *Routledge Critical Thinkers* series places key thinkers and their ideas firmly back in their contexts.

More than this, these books reflect the need to go back to the thinker's own texts and ideas. Every interpretation of an idea, even the most seemingly innocent one, offers its own 'spin', implicitly or explicitly. To read only books on a thinker, rather than texts by that thinker, is to deny yourself a chance of making up your own mind. Sometimes what makes a significant figure's work hard to approach is not so much its style or content as the feeling of not knowing where to start. The purpose of these books is to give you a 'way in' by offering an accessible overview of these thinkers' ideas and works and by guiding your further reading, starting with each thinker's own texts. To use a metaphor from the philosopher Ludwig Wittgenstein (1889–1951), these books are ladders, to be thrown away after you have climbed to the next level. Not only, then, do they equip you to approach new ideas, but also they empower you, by leading you back to a theorist's own texts and encouraging you to develop your own informed opinions.

Finally, these books are necessary because, just as intellectual needs have changed, the education systems around the world – the contexts in which introductory books are usually read – have changed radically, too. What was suitable for the minority higher education system of the

1960s is not suitable for the larger, wider, more diverse, high technology education systems of the twenty-first century. These changes call not just for new up-to-date introductions but new methods of presentation. The presentational aspects of *Routledge Critical Thinkers* have been developed with today's students in mind.

Each book in the series has a similar structure. They begin with a section offering an overview of the life and ideas of each thinker and explaining why she or he is important. The central section of each book discusses the thinker's key ideas, their context, evolution and reception. Each book concludes with a survey of the thinker's impact, outlining how their ideas have been taken up and developed by others. In addition, there is a detailed final section suggesting and describing books for further reading. This is not a 'tacked-on' section but an integral part of each volume. It opens with brief descriptions of the thinker's key works and concludes with information on the most useful critical works and, where appropriate, websites. This section will guide you in your reading, enabling you to follow your interests and develop your own projects. The books also explain technical terms and use boxes to describe events or ideas in more detail, away from the main emphasis of the discussion. Boxes are also used at times to highlight definitions of terms frequently used or coined by a thinker. In this way, the boxes serve as a kind of glossary, easily identified when flicking through the book.

The thinkers in the series are 'critical' for three reasons. First, they are examined in the light of subjects which involve criticism: principally literary studies or English and cultural studies, but also other disciplines which rely on the criticism of books, ideas, theories and unquestioned assumptions. Second, they are critical because studying their work will provide you with a 'tool kit' for your own informed critical reading and thought, which will make you critical. Third, these thinkers are critical because they are crucially important: they deal with ideas and questions which can overturn conventional understandings of the world, of texts, of everything we take for granted, leaving us with a deeper understanding of what we already knew and with new ideas.

No introduction can tell you everything. However, by offering a way into critical thinking, this series hopes to begin to engage you in an activity which is productive, constructive and potentially life-changing.

ABBREVIATIONS

BR   *The Blanchot Reader*, ed. M. Holland (Blackwell, Oxford, 1995)

DS   Maurice Blanchot, *Death Sentence*, trans. Lydia Davis (Station Hill Press, Barrytown, NT, 1978)

F   Maurice Blanchot, *Friendship*, trans. E. Rottenberg (Stanford University Press, Stanford, 1997)

FP   Maurice Blanchot, *Faux Pas* (Gallimard, Paris, 1943)

IC   Maurice Blanchot, *The Infinite Conversation*, trans. S. Hanson (University of Minnesota Press, Minneapolis, 1993)

ICN   Jean-Luc Nancy, *The Inoperative Community* (University of Minnesota Press, Minneapolis, 1991)

L   *Lignes*, Revue No. 11 (Paris, September 1990)

LS   Maurice Blanchot, *Lautréamont et Sade* (Minuit, Paris, 1963)

LV   Maurice Blanchot, *Le Livre à venir* (Gallimard, Paris, 1959)

SBR   *The Station Hill Blanchot Reader*, ed. G. Quasha (Station Hill Press, Barrytown, NY, 1999)

SL   Maurice Blanchot, *The Space of Literature*, trans. A. Smock (University of Nebraska Press, Lincoln, 1982)

SNB   Maurice Blanchot, *The Step not Beyond*, trans. L. Nelson (State University of New York Press, Albany, 1992)

SS   Maurice Blanchot, *The Siren's Song*, ed. G. Josipovici, trans. S. Rabinovitch (The Harvester Press, Brighton, 1982)

TO   Maurice Blanchot, *Thomas the Obscure* (Station Hill Press, Barrytown, NY, 1988)

UC   Maurice Blanchot, *The Unavowable Community* trans. P. Joris (Station Hill Press, Barrytown, NY, 1988)

WD   Maurice Blanchot, *The Writing of Disaster*, 2nd edition, trans. A. Smock (University of Nebraska Press, Lincoln, 1995)

WF   Maurice Blanchot, *The Work of Fire*, trans. C. Mandell (Stanford University Press, Stanford, CA, 1995)

WHY BLANCHOT?

The French writer and theorist Maurice Blanchot is one of the most important figures of the twentieth century. He has perhaps more than anyone else looked at literature as a serious philosophical question. We do not find in his work and analyses of texts any dubious statements about the value of works, whether this novel is better than that one, or whether this novelist can be ranked higher than another; rather his writing continually circles around the same question of the possibility of literature and the specific demand that literature poses to thought. It is through this insistent meditation on the possibility of literature that Blanchot has influenced a whole generation of contemporary French theorists, such as Jacques Derrida (1930–), Paul de Man (1919–1983) and Michel Foucault (1926–84). What has come to be known as post-structuralism, which has had such a decisive impact on Anglo-American critical theory, is completely unthinkable without him.

Blanchot's writings can be divided into four types: political journalism, literary reviews, novel writing and finally a hybrid style that appears to escape any genre definition, as it is a mixture of both philosophical and literary content expressed in a highly aphoristic and enigmatic style. It might be tempting to describe these different styles chronologically. The problem with this is that the blurring of the distinction between literature, literary theory and philosophy is the *point* of Blanchot's literary theory and not merely a contingent factor of its development. And still, through all these different styles, he follows through the development of his major themes, which are literature, death, ethics and politics.

We should not, however, see these four themes as standing apart from each other. The overarching question of Blanchot's thought is the meaning and possibility of literature. He does not understand literature in terms of a canon; that is to say, a hierarchy of great works to be judged according to their relative value. As we have pointed out, it would be impossible to find detailed textual criticism in Blanchot, even when his work is more traditionally presented in terms of a study of an author. Thus, for Blanchot, literature cannot be separated off into a sphere where all that matters are questions of value and good taste, as it touches upon fundamental philosophical questions. This explains why the most important writers for Blanchot are not other literary critics, but, on the one hand, philosophers, especially G.W.F. Hegel (1770–1831), Martin Heidegger (1889–1976) and Emmanuel Levinas (1906–95), and, on the other hand, those literary writers such as the Austrian (Czech) novelist Franz Kafka (1883–1924), and the French Symbolist poet Stéphane Mallarmé (1842–98), for whom the question of literature emerges from the activity of writing.

Speaking specifically about Blanchot's approach to literature, we can summarize it as follows: the key question is not whether literary texts have a particular value or not, whether they are good or bad, are part of this or that school, or belong to the great classics, but how they bring to the fore the question of what Blanchot calls the possibility of literature. This question, for Blanchot, has to do with the way that we understand language and truth. We normally understand the literary text as communicating a 'truth' to us. The aim of literary criticism is to obtain this truth. For Blanchot, on the contrary, the importance of literature, or what he would call its 'demand', is to call this truth into question. Every literary text, to the extent that we call it 'literary', resists in its own particular way any reduction to a single interpretation or meaning. The context of this approach is to be found in German Romanticism, a literary and political movement lasting from the eighteenth century well into the nineteenth century. Blanchot here sees the *origin* of modern literary theory, because it was the first school to notice the distinct character of the modern novel which turns back upon itself and becomes its own subject. Only at this moment does literature become its *own* question, rather than the object of another discourse like philosophy or history.

This more specific approach to literature widens out when we come to look at the other themes. All of Blanchot's work, from the 1940s to the 1980s, repeatedly thinks through our relation to death. It is something that he continually comes back to throughout all his writing. In one sense, he wants to say that death is something that is experienced through the demand of literature. Not of course death in the sense of one's demise, but as the question of our own 'nothingness', of the limit of one's subjectivity. For what interests Blanchot is that the condition of literature is the undoing or dissolution of the human subject; to write is to be exposed to the anonymity of language. He wants to contrast this notion of death, as it emerges through the experience of literature, with the idea of death in philosophy. In fact, it is through this meditation on death that Blanchot draws the clearest distinction between his work and the tradition of philosophy, such that the question of literature becomes a question *to* philosophy, rather than a question *of* philosophy.

This broadening out of the question of literature also links to the third theme of ethics. Again, just as we have a tendency to understand literature in terms of values, so too does the immediacy of our relation to others become submerged in our general moral principles. The cornerstone of Blanchot's understanding of ethics is the relation to the other that exceeds anything that could be said about it, any label or categorization. The medium of this ethical relation is language, and it is here that we can see the path from ethics to literature. For both are, for Blanchot, the fundamental experience of the shattering of the unity of thought. The other exceeds any designation, just as much as the literary text refuses any reduction to a simple interpretation. Language then becomes the experience of the loss of the mastery of the self.

From here there is only one further step to the question of politics, of a community which, for Blanchot, is essentially a literary community. Here Blanchot sees the major danger of our age in the way that we dissolve any important part of our lives into objectified knowledge. Yet, as neither literature, nor death, nor the other can be made into objects, we live in danger of losing the human community and, subsequently, ourselves. Blanchot thus develops the thought of the literary community (in both his published books and in his political engagement in the form of journal essays) as a way to escape this reduction of human life. Here it becomes clear that we cannot exist unless we understand our community in its literary essence. In the period from the 1950s to the 1980s, Blanchot developed this thought in the direction of the unity of Judaism, Communism and literature.

Blanchot's dedication to the cause of literature, despite his political engagement which would seem to demand a public presence, has always meant for him that the author should vanish so that the work comes to stand on its own. There is, then, something ironic in writing about the life of someone whose work demands the disappearance of the writer. With Blanchot, however, our curiosity faces not only a theoretical but a practical impossibility. For we know almost nothing at all about his life, apart from some tantalizing facts that have emerged (in many cases from Blanchot himself) in recent years. His anonymity and virtual invisibility have paradoxically increased his public fame. Here we have a French intellectual who seems not to court publicity. He writes his books and that is all. He is concretely what his theory expresses abstractly, an author who has disappeared; so that when a rumour spreads on the Internet that there is a photograph of Blanchot (can we be certain that it is him?) everyone wants to own a copy so as to make real what is only a name.

With these important qualifications in mind, let us say something briefly about what we do know about Blanchot's life. He was born on 22 September 1907 in the village of Quain in the region of Bourgogne, in eastern France. In the 1930s he wrote for extreme right-wing newspapers. It is this period of Blanchot's output that has caused the most controversy and anguish for commentators. These papers were both anti-Communist and anti-capitalist. They saw both as an embodiment of a materialist culture whose ruling law was the economy. They sought to replace the tyranny of the market with that of the state. Not a state, however, that was legitimated by the law, but through myth and the traditions of a nation, and the biological purity of a race. Inseparable from this type of nationalism is anti-Semitism, for the Jew is seen as someone who belongs to no nation, and whose existence corrupts the purity of every other race.

Was Blanchot himself anti-Semitic, simply because he was associated with these newspapers? What might cause us to hesitate in answering yes to this question is his friendship with the Jewish philosopher Emmanuel Levinas whom he met as a student at Strasbourg

University in 1927. This does not alter the fact, however, that the papers that Blanchot wrote for did publish anti-Semitic material, and he was certainly not unaware of this. The next question, and one that is perhaps more fundamental, is whether the fact that he wrote for these papers invalidates everything else that he has written. It is significant that Blanchot makes no attempt to apologize for these publications, nor does he attempt to hide his own involvement. His recent comments in letters only go so far as to correct certain inaccuracies of the historical reports of this involvement. The difficulty with dismissing Blanchot's work or reducing its significance to these biographical facts is that it runs counter to the lessons of his own work, that the impact of a text cannot be referred back to the author's life. Moreover, it makes impossible the more profound discussion of the political in Blanchot's work, where we would argue that the myth of the nation, sustained in his earlier right-wing Monarchism, is subjected to a substantial critique. Our obsession with information and facts, like Blanchot's photograph, as though we could make the 'name' real, as though all our words were as substantial as the things that surround us, can act as great hindrance to thinking about these matters in a deeper way. This is not, however, to deny Blanchot's ethical responsibility.

Blanchot's war years in Paris, like those of many of his generation, are shrouded in mystery. In these years three events stand out as being important. He saved Levinas's family from transportation to a concentration camp (Levinas himself was a prisoner of war and was spared the death camps because he was a soldier in the French army). He met and became a loyal friend of the writer Georges Bataille (1897–1962), who, like Levinas, was to have an enormous influence on his work. And, like Dostoyevsky, he appeared to undergo a transfiguring experience whilst facing a mock execution by a German firing squad. Blanchot tells us of this real or fictional event in a recent narrative *The Instant of my Death* (1994).

After the war, he returned to writing for journals such as *L'Arche*, which was one of the first independent journals at the time, edited by the French writer André Gide (1869–1951) and the philosopher and writer Jean-Paul Sartre (1905–80), and the influential *Les Temps Modernes*, which was edited by Sartre and Maurice Merleau-Ponty. His most important work, however, was published for Bataille's journal *Critique*. The war had meant a break with his political writing of the 1930s and he did not return to it. In 1947, Blanchot left Paris for

Èze-ville, a small village in south-east France on the Mediterranean coast between Nice and Monte Carlo. The years between 1940 and 1950 saw the appearance of five major novels, although many had been written previously, and, in the decade that followed, most of his narratives were published. In 1953, the most influential literary journal of France, the *Nouvelle Revue Française*, reappeared, having been closed down at the end of the war. Until 1968, there were regular monthly contributions by Blanchot, mostly in the form of book reviews, to this journal. Nearly all his critical works on literature are re-publications of this material. It is from this platform that Blanchot began to have such an extraordinary influence on French intellectual life.

In 1957, Blanchot returned to Paris. If his leaving this city ten years earlier had led to him turning his attention to literature, absorbing himself both in his own writing and the work of others, then his return marked a re-awakening of the political activities that had characterized his life in the 1930s. Now, however, it was not the politics of the extreme right wing, but the radical left. He joined the intellectual movement against de Gaulle in the 1950s. In 1960, he was one of the signatories, who were threatened with jail, of the 'manifeste des 121' against the Algerian War. In 1968, in the famous student upheavals in Paris, he was a member of the 'Comité d'action étudiants-écrivains' most of whose pamphlets were supposed to have been written by him. He later broke away from this group because of its apparent anti-Zionism. For Blanchot, the horror of the Holocaust, the extermination of 6 million Jews, hangs over every responsible thinker. His meditation on the significance of this event was strengthened and deepened by his friendship, from 1958, with Robert Antelme, who had written about his experience in the camps. Blanchot's last major work, *The Writing of Disaster* (1980) was written in its shadow. After 1968, he disappeared almost entirely from the public arena and his output gradually diminishes. His last published work appeared in 1996. He still lives in Paris and even now refuses to give interviews or make any public appearances.

This book is organized around the four main themes that we have identified. Chapters 1 and 2 discuss Blanchot's approach to literature, Chapters 3 and 4 the centrality of the theme of death, Chapter 5 the ethical relation and its connection with literature, while Chapters 6 to 8 concern themselves with his political thought. This division into themes is our own work and not Blanchot's. Thus, across his work one does not find a chapter on death or politics, in which he will discuss this theme in a general way and differentiate his own position from that of other theorists, and still less would one expect a book on one of these themes. Blanchot does not write in an 'academic' style, even in those works that one might like to call theoretical, rather each one of his pieces, which, we should never forget, were originally published in the form of literary reviews, starts with an author's name or a work, and then advances to the question of the possibility of literature. In fact there is a remarkable consistency of style in Blanchot's work, and he continually comes back to the same questions even though through different writers or works. This is also why it is difficult to speak of the development of Blanchot's work. What marks it is its stubborn refusal to let go of the question of the possibility of literature. Thus, even though one might say that his later work becomes more concerned with politics and ethics, even these topics are thought through in the context of the question of the possibility of literature. And it is this way of thinking about literature in general, though one can only approach it through a writer or a work, that is Blanchot's most important legacy to critical theory. Finally, for all these reasons, it is also difficult to say which are the key texts of Blanchot's career. For each text repeats the same questions. However, one might add, that if one wants to experience the full scope of Blanchot's critical writing, and perhaps these works are his most influential, then one might begin with *The Work of Fire* (1949), *The Space of Literature* (1955) and *The Writing of Disaster* (1980). This book is intended only as an introduction to Blanchot's work in the ways that it is relevant to critical theory. For this reason, we have made one important decision: to focus on the theoretical texts and only refer to Blanchot's literary output to the extent that it illuminates them. The further reading that we give at the end of this book also reflects this decision. As with any introduction, we hope that it will inspire the reader to go back to the original, rather than think that this book could stand in as its impossible substitute.

KEY IDEAS

1

WHAT IS LITERATURE?

If you are someone who enjoys reading fiction, then the question 'What is literature?' will probably one day come into your mind. This question seems fairly clear and no more difficult than 'What is a dog?' or 'What is a tree?' We might suggest, for example, the following definition: literature is a form of writing, whether in prose or verse, that is recognized for its creative and imaginative value. Not everyone will agree with this and some might suggest alternatives, but in arguing about definitions in this way, we are assuming that it is actually possible to define the term 'literature'.

It is this assumption which Blanchot would wish us to question. The uniqueness of his critical work is that he does not offer us one more definition of literature, which we might compare favourably or not to others, rather he argues that the process of defining this term is fraught with difficulty. A good example of this would be his debate with the French philosopher Jean-Paul Sartre (1905–80). In 1947, Sartre published a highly influential book called *What is Literature?*, which argued that the function of the writer was to engage in the political struggles of history. Blanchot's response, in his essay 'Literature and the Right to Death' (originally published in two parts in 1947–8; in SBR 359–99 and WF 300–44), which perhaps marks the beginning point of his own literary criticism, is highly ambiguous. He seems, first of all, to be offering an opposing definition of literature: literature has its own meaning that has nothing at all to do with morality and politics. We should, however, be wary of such simple oppositions. For even the critic who asserts literature's aesthetic independence is still giving a general definition of literature. Is this not what our own definition proposes? And what we have already said that Blanchot would reject? His approach is less ambitious and more uncertain. He does not deny the possibility of literary theory, which explains why he does not get involved in polemics, but argues that the experience of reading escapes *any* theory or definition, whatever form these might take. For this reason, we should not be so ready to *directly* attach literature to a political movement (although this does not mean that literature has no relation to politics, as we shall see in Chapters 6 to 8). This idea of constant 'escape' from definition leads Blanchot to write with some irony that the essence of literature is that it has no essence:

> But the essence of literature is precisely to evade any essential characteriza-tion, any affirmation which would stabilize or even realize it: it is never already there, it is always to be rediscovered or reinvented. It is never even certain that the words 'literature' or 'art' correspond to anything real, anything possible, or anything important.
>
> (BR 141)

We say 'with irony', because to say that literature has no definition is still to define literature. Rather than simply accepting this contradic-tion at face value, thereby believing we have somehow refuted Blanchot, we need to look more closely at the problem. This chapter will turn first to the general problem of defining literature. In order to understand Blanchot's position more fully, we will then consider three types of theory, in each case contrasting these with Blanchot's 'anti-theory of literature'.

DEFINITIONS

When we define something we usually do so through differentiation. This means simply that we try to pick out the characteristic or charac-teristics of a thing that make it *different* from every other thing. For example, we say that the human being belongs to the genus animal, but has the particular mark of rational thought that differentiates it from any other animal. Blanchot's argument would not be that it is impos-sible to classify literature in this way. It would be quite absurd to say that we cannot identify different kinds of literature (romance, detective story, crime thriller and so on), and similarly absurd perhaps to deny that there is no difference between literature and other forms of writing, such as police reports or newspaper articles, for example. Rather his position is that while we have little difficulty in producing definitions, the generalization that the act of definition seems to demand misses what is peculiar to the experience of reading, and, more importantly, misses what is literary about the literary text. The general philosophical definition of literature, whether defined intrinsically in terms of artistic value or extrinsically in terms of moral purpose, has nothing to do with reading. Both define literature, so to speak, from the outside. We do not read literature in general, but a particular work: Blanchot's own *Death Sentence*, say, or Emily Brontë's *Wuthering Heights*. We can say all manner of general things about these texts. We can compare and contrast them with other books, talk of them being revolutionary or conservative, belonging to this or that movement, and even label them as being included in one genre or another. None of this talk is false for Blanchot, but it skews us away from the specific experience of reading *Death Sentence* or *Wuthering Heights*, where each novel, in its own way, resists any attempt to be comprehended completely. Thus I can say, for example, that Blanchot's *Death Sentence* evokes the unsettling atmosphere of Paris during the German occupation, where all the moral certainties of French society are threatened, and yet at the same time I have the nagging doubt that I have not said anything about the novel at all. In the end we cannot say what each of these works *is*. Such opacity belongs intrinsically to the experience of reading a work and it is this singular experience which, Blanchot argues, escapes definition. It is not enough to say that literature in general repels comprehension, but that each work does so in its own manner, and thus must reinvent literature for itself.

There exists a whole industry of literary criticism and critical theory, but these books about books and words about words never seem to get any closer to the mysterious, opaque and unsettling centre of the experience of reading. The closer you feel you are approaching the centre of the work, its meaning or message, the further the work seems to withdraw from you. You feel that the text has something to say, that it has a 'truth' that can be communicated, but when you listen to the experts telling you what it means, it does not seem to capture what is truly singular about the work, for what the work communicates is only itself. For example, you might read in a critical work that the stories of Franz Kafka or Samuel Beckett are about the emptiness and senselessness of modern existence, but the critics seem to be saying both too much and too little. Every book demands an interpretation, this is the centre that attracts us, but at the same time the more that we seek this centre the more uncertain and opaque it becomes:

> A book, even a fragmentary one, has a center which attracts it. This center is not fixed, but is displaced by the pressure of the book and circumstances of its composition. Yet it is also a fixed center which, if it is genuine, displaced itself, while remaining the same and becoming always more hidden, more uncertain and more imperious.
>
> (SL v)

So how do we relate to or try to comprehend a text and at the same time always fail? Blanchot describes this text as having two sides. On one side, the text is part of our culture, and it is this aspect of the text which is the object of literary theory and it is on this aspect that critics offer their interpretations and judgements. On the other side of the text, which for Blanchot constitutes its claim to uniqueness, it speaks only in its own voice and in so doing resists our attempt to conceptualize it. It invents, so to speak, a new language that exceeds the boundaries of our critical competence. Blanchot uses the biblical story of the resurrection of Lazarus to describe these two sides. The reader is like Jesus who stands in front of the tomb and utters the command 'Lazarus come forth'. The tomb represents the book, and Lazarus the meaning of the book that the reader expects to reveal in the act of reading. There are, however, two sides to the Lazarus who emerges from the tomb: there is the resurrected Lazarus who stands there in the whiteness of the winding sheet, and there is the Lazarus whose body beneath the winding sheet still smells of the decomposing corpse of the tomb (IC 35–6 and WF 326–8). The resurrected Lazarus signifies the cultural side of the text, which allows it to be made part of the general circulation of interpretations. This side of the text is what we call its meaning or its value. The other Lazarus, who is always obscured by the resurrected Lazarus, and who never sees the light of day, depicts the opacity at the centre of every text, what remains after every interpretation, and which, like the secret of the tomb itself, refuses our grasp.

The resistance of the text to interpretation stems from the individuality of its idiom, and it is this individuality that makes the general definition of literature impossible for Blanchot. What is important, however, is not to let the two sides of literature fall into an empty opposition. The irreducibility of the text, its stubborn individuality, is only revealed through reading and through the failure of interpretation, not in opposition to it. But how and why does the text avoid the intention of the reader to comprehend it? To answer this question we can compare Blanchot's approach to literature with other influential critical positions, if only very briefly. This will reveal more clearly the originality of his stance.

LITERARY THEORIES

The development of Blanchot's thought cannot be separated from the mode of its presentation. Nearly all of his critical works are collections of reviews first published in journals such as the *Journal des Débats*, *Critique* and *La Nouvelle Revue Française*. Journals of this type are perhaps specific to the French intellectual milieu. They are a kind of combination of the literary pages of a newspaper and an academic journal, but what is most important is that they are independent of academia. Their existence not only allowed Blanchot a means of living, but also an independence of thought. Thus, unlike most literary critics, he has written no substantial work in which he presents his own views or criticizes those of others. These reviews, and as time passes they resemble even this form less and less, are almost completely devoid of footnotes, and make hardly any references to his contemporaries, with a few notable exceptions, such as Georges Bataille and Emmanuel Levinas. This form of presentation makes it extremely difficult to reconstruct Blanchot's thought and to trace the influences on this work. One way of countering this problem is to imagine Blanchot in dialogue with the main strains of literary theory and to imagine, on the basis of the work that we have, the objections he might raise in regard to them. Our intention is not to be exhaustive, but to consider three types of theory in comparison to Blanchot's approach. Each of these types of theory concentrates on the three main elements of literature: the author, the reader and the text.

LITERATURE AS BIOGRAPHY

If you were reading a literary text, you might be tempted to say that the purpose of the text was to communicate what was in the writer's mind when he or she first wrote it. Let us say you are reading James Joyce's *Ulysses* (1922). You might want to say that the text was essentially a translation of the inner mind of the writer into an outer, external form. The different characters and situations, then, would merely be different aspects of the writer's mind. You might even claim that the text could translate the writer's unconscious. For example, the text of *Ulysses* might contain unconscious ideological material, such as the class-consciousness of intellectuals in the early part of the twentieth century, of which the writer, James Joyce, was not even aware. This notion of the writer's unconscious can yield a very broad scope for interpretation, then, from the individual psychology of writer to the mass psychology of a society. The object of this kind of commentary would be to get as close as possible to the writer's original thoughts and intentions, or, and this is undoubtedly very difficult, to hidden unconscious meaning and its repression. Once such a commentary had located this material it would claim that it had discovered the 'truth' of the text, which would have been concealed from more 'naïve' readings.

The literary criticism we have in mind here is that inspired by the works of Freud. Blanchot too writes about Freud, but he is not at all inspired to find hidden meanings (IC 230–7). How can we imagine him responding to such a theory of textual meaning? He would probably ask how we are to know what the original intentions of the author might have been. This complication is further compounded if we start talking of the author's unconscious translated into the text. Even if the author is still alive to attest to the supposed meaning behind the text, how can we be certain that their judgements about their own work are valid? The only way to determine this would be to judge the work for yourself, but this is precisely what is ruled out by saying that the meaning of a text lies in the intentions of the author.

SIGMUND FREUD (1856–1939)

A Viennese neurologist who discovered, in treating his patients for nervous disorders, unconscious thought processes and a new method of psychoanalysis in order to analyse them. For the purposes of literary criticism, his most influential idea was the distinction between the latent and manifest content of dreams that he outlined in his major work *The*

Interpretation of Dreams (1900), where the manifest content referred to the surface material of the dream, the apparent illogical associations of images, and the latent content to that which had to be teased out by interpretation. One such example of the relation between manifest and latent content was dream symbolism, where an object in a dream might represent an erotized body part or activity, though one must be wary of overemphasizing the importance of this symbolism for Freud. In his own interpretation of the work of literary authors, Freud tended to interpret in relation to the writer's life, as though they were his patients. Blanchot does not write directly on Freudian interpretation, but does discuss psychoanalysis in the essay 'Analytic Speech' (IC 342–54).

READERS' RESPONSE

It is not at all clear that the writer is the best judge of their work, and when a writer does judge his or her own work, as Blanchot reminds us, he or she is no longer its writer, but merely its first reader. As such, authors have no more direct access to the work than the readers who follow (SL 200–1). Their closeness to the work might blind them to its full significance. Moreover, are we so certain that all the meanings of a text are to be found in the original intentions of the author who wrote it? Does not a text have many more possibilities than this? Just think, for example, of those texts whose authorship is uncertain. Would we say that these texts have no meaning, because we have no knowledge of the people who wrote them? Or, again, imagine the possibility that the name on the front of a book you were reading disappeared, and all knowledge about that author with it. Would you be certain that when you opened that book the pages would be a blank for you, and that you would no longer understand a word?

Maybe it is the case that what you say about the author's intentions is just your own opinion disguised by another's name and this is a necessary outcome of every interpretation. This is why we might think that it is the reader who activates the meaning of the text by pouring his or her own life into it, without which the text would be dead and lifeless. Thus, the meaning of the literary text, to go back to our first example of James Joyces's *Ulysses*, lies neither in the writer's mind, nor in the text itself, but in the *interaction* between the reader and the text. For this reason, we could say that any text has multiple meanings and that interpretations of it will be as varied as the people who read it. Each reader brings his or her own values or opinions to a book, consciously or unconsciously, and what that book means to that reader will be coloured by these preconceived ideas. Readers may not even be aware of this: their social positions might tie them into whole cultural attitudes that they unknowingly express in their interpretations of a book. The object of the literary critic would then be not to find the 'truth' of the work, which would somehow mysteriously lie outside of time, but to trace the history of its reception. For example, the themes that we pick out in Shakespeare today would be quite different from those that interested his first audience, but we cannot claim that either response is truer than the other.

The literary school roughly described here is known as reader response or reception theory, stressing in its label the contribution of the reader to the understanding of the literary text. We could imagine Blanchot's reply to this theory to be that it fails to pay sufficient attention to the way in which the text, just as much as it invites readers in, also dismisses them. However much the reader draws close to the text, it also remains outside them in its own stubborn isolation. The text's resistance to appropriation by the reader does not signify that the text is meaningless, but precisely the opposite: this resistance is the significance of the text and it is this resistance that makes the text literary. Another way of putting this would be to say that a text is literary to the extent that it says more than we can comprehend, but this 'more' is not experienced merely negatively as an absence of meaning, but as excess of meaning. This is what we mean by the strange particular and individual world or style of a work, one that resists any general categorization or label.

RECEPTION THEORY

A theory of literature that concentrates on the reader's role in the production of the meaning of a text and which came out of the University of Constance in Germany. Some of the major names of this movement are Hans Robert Jauss, Wolfgang Iser and Peter Szondi. Reception theory lays stress upon the historical dimension of literary texts, but concentrates more on the reader than the author as the origin of its meaning. Thus, a text can change meaning across history and across different communities. There is no ultimate meaning of Shakespeare, for example, that would stand above the historical and social context of its consumption. Blanchot makes no specific comment upon reception theory, but, although he would not deny the historical and social nature of reading, he would withstand the reduction of the 'literary space' to merely one more item of 'culture'. What interests him is precisely the resistance of the text to the reader's response, as for example in the essay 'The Great Reducers' (F 62–72). We shall discuss this essay in Chapter 7.

STRUCTURALISM

Another way of interpreting literature would be neither to focus on the writer or the reader, but on the text. Such an approach to literature was theorized in the 1920s in what is now known as the Russian Formalist School, often seen as the progenitor of modern critical theory. The formalists' aim was to return to the text as the proper object of the study of literature, against the vogue for psychological, sociological and historical interpretations. This school of theory says that we can safely ignore the fact that the literary text was written by this or that person and claims that all that matters is just the text that is present to us in the act of reading. It would make no difference to the *meaning* of *Ulysses* if we were to erase the name 'James Joyce' from the front cover of the book. Or else, rather than losing the author's name completely, it might be said that when we speak about literary texts the author's name no longer refers to the real person, but is merely the label for a body of work: the collection of works that stand on our library shelves under the label 'Joyce'. It would be absurd to look for the actual Joyce there, the one who really was born in Ireland, who really did walk the streets of Dublin and who really exiled himself to mainland Europe. The text is much more and much less than this reality. This does not mean that these elements cannot be found in Joyce's work, but as part of this work they have undergone a transformation, which means that they are no longer aspects of the real world. To treat literature as though it was nothing but an historical or biographical document is to ignore this difference completely.

What we will find, critics of this school might say, if we start with the text itself, and not with the supposition that it is merely the contents of the writer's or reader's mind, are structures and arrangements of the written word that are repeated not just through the writer's own work and the reader's own response to it, but across different writers, works and even separate cultures. These structures or models can be analysed objectively, because their existence belongs neither to the intentions of the writer, nor to the inclinations of the reader. They exist, so to speak, outside of them both, shaping and determining every act of creation and reading.

Blanchot is perhaps closest to the last position, for he too believes that the text is autonomous. It is also true that at the time when he was developing his theories, structuralism, which is the particularly French version of formalism, was very popular. It is, however, far too simple to call Blanchot a formalist as the structuralist interpretation of the text, as it was practised, for example, by the French anthropologist, Claude Lévi-Strauss (1908–), aims to demonstrate a common framework underlying every text. It therefore takes a *general* approach, seeking to discover what is common or shared by different works of art. Blanchot's argument for literature's autonomy, on the contrary, concerns the absolute *singularity* of the work. This means that for Blanchot the obligation of the literary critic is not to find the essence of the text, and through that essence a general theory of literature, but to follow the individual lines and traits of the text. This process would eventually lead the critic, as Blanchot remarks in his book on the writings of Lautréamont (1846–70) and the Marquis de Sade (1740–1814), to losing the text itself: 'We would wish simply to experience to what extent one can follow a text and at the same time lose it' (LS 59). The object of criticism is not to make the text more transparent and intelligible, but more difficult and impervious by demonstrating that it exceeds every interpretation, even its own self-interpretation. This means, for Blanchot, that the critic has a double duty. He or she has to interpret the text, but also to show that this interpretation does not work. In the formalist or structuralist position, language is a means to explanation, whereas for Blanchot the language of literature is the impediment to every explanation: 'Literature indeed remains the object of critique, but critique does not manifest literature' (LS 9).

FROM RUSSIAN FORMALISM TO FRENCH STRUCTURALISM

The formalist school of literary criticism came from Russia in the first half of the twentieth century. It stressed that the proper object of the study of literature was the autonomy of the text as against it being merely the image of the author's life or the product of a reader's culture. The autonomy of the text was understood to lie in the particular form of literary language that distinguished it from ordinary language, and the aim of many formalist studies was to describe and analyse these effects. Formalist methodology found its way into structuralism through the work of Claude Lévi-Strauss but was also combined with a heavy emphasis on structural linguistics that emerged from the work of the Swiss linguist Ferdinand de Saussure (1857–1913). The aim of structuralism is to analyse the totality of language rather than specific instances, and it does so through the description of the codes of a discourse, but, unlike formalism, it does not isolate these codes from their social context. The aim of a structuralist interpretation of a text is not to demonstrate what a text means but to show how the elements with text work in their relation to one another. Of all the approaches to literature it is perhaps to these two movements that Blanchot is the closest. His distance from them, and this distance is very important, is the insistence that what makes a literary text work after all is that it never works as well as it should; that is to say, that it always exceeds any interpretation that would hope to make the text perfectly present. Again, like all these literary theories, Blanchot does not write directly upon either formalism or structuralism, but to get some idea about Blanchot's own understanding of literary language and the similarity and difference of his stance from formalism and structuralism, one could not do better than to start with the essay 'The Pursuit of the Zero Point' (BR 143–50).

BLANCHOT'S ANTI-THEORY OF LITERATURE

In his earliest essays and book reviews, Blanchot repeats over and over again that what matters in our understanding of a text are not the original writer's intentions or beliefs, nor our own subjective responses, but rather the text's stubborn independence. He draws our attention to the independence or 'separateness' of the text from our own world.

Our ordinary relation to literature is to try and draw the text into our everyday world, reducing it to our feelings and opinions. We end up treating the characters in novels as though they were real people, imagining them to be just like ourselves with the same feelings, opinions and beliefs, and as though they could make decisions and choices in their lives. We forget that we are reading literature. We read the text as though it were real, and are inattentive to the fact that the reality of a novel is merely an illusion that words make possible. Or we use literature as a kind of therapy for our own emotional or psychological problems. Worst of all, perhaps, literature becomes only a means to entertain ourselves.

Likewise, when we identify the text with the life of the author who has written it, are we not also trying to make it less alien and strange, for is not the author a human being like us who has the same worries and desires, but merely has the talent to express in words what we confusedly feel? In each case, whether we reduce the literary text to the inner life of the reader, who identifies with the characters or situations of the novel, or to that of the writer, as though the very same characters or situations were only the external manifestation of his or her inner life, we forget that what is central to the experience of reading is a language that precisely *distances* us from life. The text, in the very manner of its presentation, opens a space between it and the world. It is this space that is closed down when we say, for example, that Samuel Beckett's novels are merely about the emptiness and absurdity of modern life. For such an interpretation overlooks that what is essential to literature is the estrangement of its language from ordinary usage.

> In poetry we are no longer referred back to the world, neither to the world as shelter nor to the world as goals. In this language the world recedes and goals cease; the world falls silent; beings with their preoccupations, their projects, their activity are no longer ultimately what speaks …. Then language takes on all of its importance. It becomes essential. Language speaks as the essential, and that is why the word entrusted to the poet can be called the essential word.

> (SL 41)

The language of literature is not the same as the language of communication. Every individual literary text, whether we are speaking of a novel or a poem, has its own autonomy and no general description could capture the uniqueness of its expression. Indeed, for Blanchot, the criterion of being literary is this singularity or separateness, which he calls in *The Space of Literature* the 'solitude' of the work of art (SL 21–2). It is this difference that goes some way to explain the originality of Blanchot's literary criticism and his influence on subsequent French critical theorists like Jacques Derrida. For where the formalist or structuralist critic looks for 'essences' that lie beneath the individual works of art and which therefore can act as a means of comparing one work to another, the autonomy of the work of art, for Blanchot, is the particular resistance of any text, because of the very density of its language, to any interpretation and thus to any general definition. Again, it is not that Blanchot is arguing that one could not give a definition of literature; rather, such definitions seem to miss what is integral to reading. Ignorance belongs implicitly to it, and is not something to be overcome by the accumulation of more and more knowledge:

> Reading is ignorant. It begins with what it reads and in this way discovers the force of a beginning. It is receiving and hearing, not the power to decipher and analyze, to go beyond by developing or to go back before by laying bare; it does not comprehend (strictly speaking), it attends. A marvelous innocence.

> (IC 320)

SUMMARY

If Blanchot can be said to have a theory of literature, it is, paradoxically, an *anti-theory*. For him the experience of reading is *singular* and texts resist a final and closed interpretation. Reading and texts, therefore, escape all definition of literature and literary theories, as these work by generalizations. We can compare Blanchot's approach with other literary theories that attempt to set the literary text within some kind of general background and to locate its 'meaning' in the *author*, the *reader* or the *text*. For Blanchot, however, one side of the text, which stands apart from its possession as cultural object, always resists codification or categorization and this is what is central to the experience of reading. The key to understanding the text's resistance is *language*: the language of literature is estranged from its ordinary usage and no general description could capture the uniqueness of a text's expression.

2

LANGUAGE AND LITERATURE

It is not enough simply to say that literature resists comprehension, we have to explain why. We have already alluded to the importance of Blanchot's essay 'Literature and the Right to Death' as the key to understanding his anti-theory of literature (p. 11). What is at the heart of this essay, and is continually repeated throughout Blanchot's work, is the link between language and negativity, where negativity describes the power of language to negate the reality of things through the insubstantiality of the word. The context of this idea is not other literary theorists but philosophy, and in this particular case the idea of negativity as it is presented in the work of the German philosopher G.W.F. Hegel (1770–1831); or, to be more precise, the philosophy of Hegel as it is presented by the Russian émigré philosopher Alexander Kojève (1902–68), whose lectures on Hegel not only decisively influenced Blanchot's ideas on literature, but a whole generation of French intellectuals. We shall also see that for Blanchot this Hegelian conception of language is strongly mediated by the remarks on language and poetry by the French Symbolist poet Stéphane Mallarmé (1842–98).

In this chapter we shall first look at a model of the common conception of language, which we will then compare to literature. We shall be able to see that for Blanchot the language of literature in his earlier writings is interpreted in terms of the materiality of words (their sound, shape and rhythm) which then becomes developed through the

Hegelian notion of negativity into a meditation upon the absence at the heart of the literary word.

THE INFORMATIONAL MODEL OF LANGUAGE

Let us first turn to the poet Stéphane Mallarmé whose influence on Blanchot was significant, because a reflection upon the nature of language was central to his own practice and thinking about poetry. This does not mean that he wrote a systematic study of language from which his followers could develop a conclusive theory. Blanchot is quite adamant that we should not consider Mallarmé's remarks on language to be a theory in the sense of a linguistic science and even his supposedly 'theoretical' remarks are as indirect and enigmatic as his poetry (WF 29).

STÉPHANE MALLARMÉ

Mallarmé's collected works comprise one single volume, but his influence on contemporary literary criticism is almost without comparison. References to his work are numerous in the works of such writers as Roland Barthes, Michel Foucault, Jacques Lacan and Jacques Derrida. It would not be an exaggeration to say that Mallarmé's reflections upon language and poetry are the seed for postmodern literary theory. He worked as an English teacher in several *lycées* (state secondary schools) in France, but during the evenings would write poetry or converse with other poets in his famous Tuesday evening meetings. This group of friends came to be known as the 'Symbolists' and it was perhaps Mallarmé's work itself that captured in essence this symbolist style with its emphasis on the literary effects of language as opposed to its representational function. Two of the most important works of Mallarmé are the poem 'A Roll of the Dice' (1914) and the essay 'Crisis in Poetry' (1897). In the former, the typographical lay-out of the poem is as important as the words on the page, where the work refers neither to author, nor the external world, but to the impermanent presence of the written word, and in the latter, Mallarmé, in a series of aphorisms, alludes enigmatically to his own theories of literature and language. His importance to postmodernism lies in this emphasis upon the textuality of language as opposed to its ability to represent the world, to such an extent that representation itself is merely seen as a result of textuality.

Blanchot takes from Mallarmé a model of the common conception of language as medium for the exchange of ideas. According to this model, when I speak to you, the words that I utter voice the thoughts that are in my mind. You listen to these sounds, and if you are a competent speaker of the language, you translate them back into thoughts in your own mind. If this exchange of information is successful then the thoughts in my mind will be the same as those in yours. The written word, then, would seem to be simply the recording and storage of information to be activated at a later date by someone who reads it, if we assume that the act of 'writing down' in no way changes the function of language as this exchange of ideas. There does not seem to be any problem in applying this model to literature; it appears as the simple exchange of a messages.

What seems to us a rather obvious interpretation of language, however, rests upon a particular model that needs to be investigated more deeply. In this model, language is made up of the three following components: the material medium, the mental concept and the thing referred to. With these very elementary distinctions we can come to a basic and rudimentary definition of the informational model of language as follows: it is the passage of information from one mind to another via a material medium that expresses a mental concept or idea that refers to things in the world. To simplify, we could say that the three elements of the informational model are the word, the concept and the thing.

The question that Blanchot asks is whether the relation between these elements is the same in literary language as it is in our ordinary use of language, and the element that he focuses on first is the material medium of literature.

THE MATERIALITY OF THE WORD: MESSAGE VS MEDIUM

In the informational model of language, the spoken or written word is merely a vehicle for the meaning that it conveys. If this view is correct, what might appear to us as essential to language, namely the words themselves, their material presence, whether as the cadence of the voice or the style of the words on the page, becomes what is most inessential. This model's ideal of communication, then, would be the disappearance of the word in the pure translatability of meaning.

In the information model of language, this ideal has two forms. One form is the internal monologue of thought, where the mind directly communicates to itself without the necessity of any external medium. The second form of this would be a pure notation that would reduce the confusion of ordinary language to a minimum. For exponents of the informational model of language, words just seem to get in the way of information, and it is words, rather than the intentions of the participants, which lead to confusion and disorder in the sending of a message from one person to another. If only there could be a direct communication between minds and a pure language, then, according to this view, the worst effects of words would be minimized.

Of course this is only an ideal, but you will perhaps begin to see why this informational model of language is so inappropriate for understanding literature. For it is precisely in what this ideal wishes to eliminate that the significance of literature lies. Without words literature is nothing. Not simply because literature would no longer mean anything in the absence of words, for this is also true in the case of the informational model of language, but because in literature it is not only the meaning of words which matters, but their *texture*, which is to say their rhythm, colour and style, none of which can be reduced to an item of information. We need only to think of our appreciation of poetry to see that this must be so:

> We understand fairly well that the poet rejects everyday language, if the habits and determinations of active life have the effect of removing all material reality from this language. We understand also that the poet wishes to restore language to its own value, that he searches to make it visible, and to separate it from all that annuls it. That said, if it is true that poetry must be occupied with all that in words has no use, being attentive to images, number, rhythm, contour of syllable, then we have to ask what this resurrection of a language that wishes to exist as such aims at.

(FP 160)

The emphasis on the materiality of the word belongs to Blanchot's early criticism and this quotation is taken from an essay 'Poetry and Language' that was first published in 1943. It would be quite wrong to say that this is all that Blanchot has to say about the difference between literary and ordinary language. It is the question that ends this quotation that becomes the guiding force of his later writing. What is it that language aims at when it is no longer only the expression of a message?

Blanchot remarks that Mallarmé likens the ordinary use of language to the exchange of money in the market place (SL 39). Like the money that exchanges hands after a purchase, words disappear in their function, which is to stand as a representative for something else. As money merely represents the value of the goods exchanged, so words are merely the representatives of ideas. For literature, on the contrary, the very thing the exchange of information sees as unimportant, namely the material presence of words, is what is most essential, and rather than the words disappearing in the demand of reading, they remain.

Blanchot's aim in contrasting the language of literature to the language of information is not only to draw attention to this differing emphasis on the material presence of the word. What is decisive for Blanchot is the way in which this emphasis changes the relation between the word and the meaning it is supposed to express. In language understood as information, everything is subordinated to the transferability of meaning from one mind to another, whereas in literature or in what Blanchot will increasingly just call 'writing', it is not the message, but the medium that is important, and this medium can only be understood as that which resists, interrupts or suspends the message. Literature becomes what it is, rather than merely a carrier for something external, like the thoughts of an author or the meaning of a culture. This folding back of literature upon itself, which is the very definition of modernism, is conveyed most succinctly for Blanchot in Mallarmé's late poetic experiments, such as in his poem 'Un coup de dès' ('A Throw of the Dice', 1914) where the typography of the poem is an essential part of the poetic effect.

Thus, for Blanchot, the wrong way to read literature would be to read it as though it were *only* communicating a message. Unfortunately, this is often the way people do read, as though a novel or poem were little more than a psychological or historical document, whose form was of no significance at all. Or even if we do pay attention to the form of the work, then it is only again to reduce it to another meaning. This does not mean that Blanchot thinks that literature has no meaning, since we can always interpret a text, but that there is always more to literature than merely this reference that it makes to our world.

So far we have only spoken about Blanchot's project negatively; that is to say, the manner in which he thinks that literature cannot be made part of our ordinary understanding of language. In the next section, we shall move on to Blanchot's positive description of literature. This will bring us to Blanchot's meditations on literature in the essay 'Literature and the Right to Death', which has been the guiding thread of our interpretation. Again the inspiration for Blanchot is Mallarmé, who understands language as negativity. Yet Mallarmé himself obtained this idea from his reading of Hegel, which explains why this philosopher is so important to Blanchot in this essay. Nonetheless, although this idea originally comes from a philosopher, it undergoes a strange inversion in the hands of Mallarmé and Blanchot. For Hegel, negativity is the essence of language because it explains the function of the concept to negate the reality of the thing (this will be an important argument in Chapter 3, where we shall also give a fuller explanation of the meaning of this 'negativity'). But, for Blanchot and Mallarmé, this negativity is not negative enough, for the absence of the concept is redeemed by the presence of the idea. If language is negation, then it is literature that truly embodies its strange power, for it negates both the reality of the thing and the presence of the idea. It is a double absence. To make this clearer, for it is the most obscure part of Blanchot's anti-theory of literature, we shall first discuss how Mallarmé and Blanchot understand the absence of language in general and then in particular how this absence is pushed to its extreme in literature.

NEGATION AND THE ABSENCE OF LANGUAGE

What is fundamental to language for both Blanchot and Mallarmé is negation. Language only communicates the idea of something to us, because at the same time it negates the reality of the thing. In 'Literature and the Right to Death' Blanchot uses the example of saying the word 'woman':

> I say 'This woman.' Hölderlin, Mallarmé, and all poets whose theme is the essence of poetry have felt that the act of naming is disquieting and marvellous. A word may give me its meaning, but first it suppresses it. For me to be able to say, 'This woman,' I must somehow take her flesh-and-blood reality away from her, cause her to be absent, annihilate her.
>
> (WF 322)

Language communicates the meaning of woman by erasing the particularity of this actual woman, even when I point to her and say 'this woman', for the same word can be used to mean that woman standing over there or any other woman. This is the same for any word that I might use. The word 'tree' is not the same as the tree that stands in my garden, but it is also not the same as any other tree. It is the negation of all particular *real* trees for the sake of the *idea* of a tree. The essential character of language is its power of abstraction; that is to say, its *distance* from the reality of things. This distance Blanchot and Mallarmé interpret as the power of language to negate the actual, individual concrete thing, for the sake of the *idea* of a thing: in language, writes Blanchot, 'speech has a function that is not only representative but also destructive. It causes to vanish, it renders the object absent, it annihilates it' (WF 30).

What happens in the information model of language is that it forgets this essence of language. It forgets that language, even before some meaning is expressed, is this distance from things. As speaking beings we are always already banished from the immediacy of things. We are suspended in the absence of language, and this suspension is what prevents language from finding stability in an extra-linguistic reality. The word 'tree' does not ever just mean this or that tree, for it has already withdrawn itself from their reality. Even the idea tree is a poetic fragment that has forgotten its moment of creation.

According to Blanchot and Mallarmé, the absence of language is covered over or concealed by the idea or concept expressed in the word. In this case, words refer back to the things that they have negated. The disappearance of the thing is replaced by the idea, which has as much stability and constancy as the thing which was originally negated. In fact, philosophically speaking, the idea has more permanence than the thing, since the latter can always change and alter. We can define the concept, therefore, as the substitute for the thing. The concept replaces the thing that was first of all negated by the word, and as a substitute or representative of the thing, it fills in the absence left behind by the power of language to negate the immediacy of things. What is referred to in language is not the actual thing itself, but the concept or the idea of the thing. The destructive power of language is transformed into something positive, whereby the absence of the thing is replaced by the presence of the concept.

THE DOUBLE ABSENCE OF LITERATURE

In literature, however, the word does not transform the negativity of language into the positivity of the concept, but stubbornly maintains and preserves it. Such negativity, Blanchot calls the uselessness or 'worklessness' (*désœuvrement*) of the literary work. If language is understood as negativity, then it is literature rather than the exchange of information that is closer to its essence, for the latter conceals this absence, whereas literature demands that we experience this absence as absence. It does so not only by negating the reality of the thing in the word, but also the concept to which the word refers. In its ordinary use the word 'cat' just means the idea of a cat, but in literature no word just means what it says:

> To name the cat is, if you like, to make it into a non-cat, a cat that has ceased to exist, has ceased to be a living cat, but this does not mean one is making it into a dog, or even a non-dog. This is the primary difference between common language and literary language. The first accepts that once the non-existence of the cat has passed into the word, the cat itself comes to light again fully and certainly in the form of its idea (its being) and its meaning.
>
> (WF 325)

If the word, in literature, no longer refers to the thing, then what does it link to? Blanchot's answer to this question is other words, where this chain does not end up in any ultimate referent or meaning, but the absence that is at the heart of language. Take for example Mallarmé's famous 'Sonnet in yx' (1887), which seems to be about his lover's fingernails, while the rhyming scheme of words ending in 'yx' takes over any representational content the poem might have. The word comes to have a fragile presence that no longer refers to the thing or the concept, a fragile presence that is the *absence* of thing and concept. When we say that a text has a meaning, it is this absence that we are precisely recoiling from. This absence is the very stubborn but fragile presence of the word, which is endlessly re-invented in the demand of writing, in the style of a writer, at once both its materiality and insubstantiality. We can now begin to understand the origin of literature's resistance to comprehension that we discussed in the previous chapter. If the word links to another word, rather than to some idea outside the text, then what we have is not an item of information, but an infinite displacement of meaning that cannot be stabilized in a single interpretation. Blanchot describes this displacement as the power words have, when they are no longer tied to the function of the concept, of destroying themselves:

> Words, we know, have the power to make things disappear. ... But words, having the power to make things 'arise' at the heart of their absence – words which are masters of this absence – also have the power to disappear in themselves, to absent themselves marvelously in the midst of the totality which they realize, which they proclaim as they annihilate themselves therein, which they accomplish eternally by destroying themselves there endlessly.
>
> (SL 43)

The firmness of the ground beneath our feet is seemingly replaced by the infinite interconnections between words, where one word refers to another word and so on, and where they could not constitute a totality or complex of concepts that would designate a discernible reality. It is true that we might speak of the universe or world of a novel or a poem, but this universe or world is not the world or universe in which we live or exist; rather, it is the work's own world and universe, one that, unlike ours, is infinitely open, allusive and enigmatic spurring us on to endless interpretations that forever remain unsatisfied. There is a passage in the second version of Blanchot's first novel *Thomas the Obscure*, where Thomas reads a page of a book lying open in his room, that describes vividly and powerfully the effect words have when they are released from their function to designate things:

> He perceived all the strangeness there was in being observed by a word as if by a living thing, and not simply by one word, but by all the words that were in that word, by all those that went with it and in turn contained other words, like a possession of angels opening out into the infinite to the very eye of the absolute.
>
> (TO 25)

This infinite chain of words freed from the function of designation or referentiality, that emerges when the word turns back upon itself, rather than outwards to the thing, is literature's centre. Blanchot attempts to capture it in the image of a language that is spoken by no one, the 'murmur of the incessant and the interminable', and which he calls the *demand of writing* or the *worklessness of the work* (SL 48). It resists any attempt to subordinate it to a concept or a meaning. The absence of meaning at the centre of the literary text should not be interpreted as nonsense, as though literature were meaningless and did not have its own law. Not being able to reach this centre is, therefore, not to be understood as a failure upon our part, if failure is interpreted in this context as a lack of knowledge. It is not because we have too little knowledge that we cannot comprehend the text, rather the text's resistance to comprehension belongs intrinsically to the experience of reading.

This double absence of both the thing and the concept in literature means that Blanchot holds a strong anti-realist conception of literature. 'Poetry', he writes 'does not respond to the appeal of material objects. Its function is not to preserve them by naming them' (SS 228). A realist view, on the contrary, sees literature as merely a representation of the world in which we live. Thus, the places in novels are taken to be exactly the same as the places we inhabit and the characters no different from the people we speak to in our own world, with their own feelings, desires and personal tragedies. But if the power of language is to negate the real world for its own world, and if literature expresses to the greatest extent this power of language, then a novel or a poem cannot just be a description, imitation or reflection of the world. Words have the power to go beyond concepts and this is their fascination and, in the end, their duplicity and dissimulation. This does not mean that there are no realist elements in the novel or the poem, or that it has no relation to the real world at all. Rather, Blanchot speaks of there being two sides or 'slopes' to literature. On the one side, there is the realist content, which one can interpret as belonging to the social world, and, on the other, there is the purity of the language of literature itself, which folds back upon itself, so as to turn away from the everyday use of words:

> Literature is divided between these two slopes. ... The first slope is meaningful prose. Its goal is to express things in a language that designates things according to what they mean. ... But still on this side of language, there comes a moment when art realizes that everyday speech is dishonest and abandons it. What is art's complaint about everyday speech? It says it lacks meaning: art feels it is madness to think that in each word some thing is completely present through the absence that determines it, and so art sets off in quest of a

language that can recapture this absence itself and represent the endless movement of comprehension.

(WF 332–3)

What is a book? Of course, in one sense it is a thing like any other made from ink and paper and like them belongs to my everyday experience of the world. I can find books in libraries and bookstores, and they lie unopened upon my desk. What happens, however, when I open the covers of one of them and begin reading? What world am I in then? Is it still the same familiar world? One side of the book I am reading does belong to this world. I can add this book, like a record in an account register, to all the other books I have read. I can become a 'cultured' person. I can also read books about the books I have read, and gain more and more knowledge about them. Not only am I now cultured, but I am also an expert. There is, however, another side of the book, which Blanchot calls the 'work', that does not belong to this habitual world. It is the singular experience of the work as it slips away from my grasp and from which side there is no general experience of literature, since there are no concepts which would translate the impervious nature of the work without immediately placing it on the other side; that is to say, the side of culture.

We want the work to be a representation of something; we want it to mean something. Thus we want the figure of the castle in Franz Kafka's *The Castle*, for example, to be a symbol of the absolute, as though the function of the image in literature were as straightforward as the function of a concept (where 'cat' means cat). This novel was first published posthumously in 1926. Its narrative consists of a character named K. who searches endlessly for a castle. Like any novel, however, it does not work that way, or does not work at all, if 'working' here means producing a stable meaning. It is, Blanchot writes, 'infinitely more and thus also infinitely less than all of its interpretations' (IC 395). The figure of the castle, rather than being the unity of the work, an answer to the question 'What does the work mean?', is its dispersal and the experience of the absence of meaning. The castle is the centre of Kafka's novel, but just as the castle withdraws from K. as he gets nearer to it (it looks on closer inspection to be nothing more than a ramshackle collection of village buildings), so too does the centre of the work withdraw from the reader.

SUMMARY

The key to Blanchot's anti-theory of literature is language. In the widely accepted information model of language, a *message* is passed from one mind to another via a *word* that expresses a *concept* which in turn refers to a *thing* in the world. The medium (*word*) is subordinated to the message. In literature, however, or what Blanchot calls *writing*, the medium resists or interrupts the message, as the sound, texture and rhythm of words take precedence over their meaning. In literature, and here the unmistakable influence of Mallarmé is apparent, it is not so much what language expresses that is important, but language itself. Blanchot, however, takes this notion of the transformation of language in literature even further, by stressing the *negativity* and *absence* that lies at its centre. In the informational, or 'ordinary' use of language, the *word* negates the actual *thing*, but covers over this absence by referring to the *concept* of the thing. The destructive power of language is therefore changed into something positive. In literature, however, the word maintains the negativity of language, negating both the concept and thing, demanding that we experience this absence as absence. In literature, Blanchot argues, the word, freed from its function of representing the world, creates its own world in its internal linkage to other words. And yet even at the heart of this world, there is a fundamental impermanence, for there is no external reality to give it a stable meaning. On the one hand, this absence is what compels us to interpret the text, but, on the other, it is what prevents us from being finished with the act of explanation once and for all.

3

DEATH AND PHILOSOPHY

This chapter will make a necessary detour in order to further our investigation of Blanchot's work. Death is a theme that runs throughout his work and organizes his reflections on language, literature and philosophy. It is by a constant reflection on death that Blanchot, from his earliest to his latest works, takes on the tradition of Western philosophical thought, but it is also where he engages most directly with philosophy, so that it is necessary first to sketch out this philosophical thought itself. While the concept of death has played a central role in philosophy since its inception, Blanchot's discussion moves mainly between the thought of G.W.F. Hegel (1770–1831), to whom we have already referred, and that of Martin Heidegger (1889–1976), who is widely seen as one of the most original and influential philosophers of the twentieth century. The special status of these two thinkers in Blanchot's work is legitimated in that Hegel has made of death the key concept of philosophy, while Heidegger already uses his characterization of the human being as a being-towards-death as the main lever against the tradition of philosophy and the trust that it places in the power of reason.

This chapter is, then, divided into three parts. First of all, we shall generally look at the meaning of death in philosophy, then at Hegel's conception of death and finally at Heidegger's. This overview will assist us in the next chapter to see how Blanchot sets himself apart from what he considers to be the philosophical definition of death, both against its highest expression in Hegel and against the attempt of its retrieval in Heidegger. Through this discussion we will bring out the ambiguity of Blanchot's relation to philosophy. That is, while Blanchot approaches the question of literature through philosophy rather than remaining within the confines of literary theory, he does not become a philosopher writing about the possibility of literature. Rather than seeing literature as a question *of* philosophy, he understands it as a question posed *to* philosophy.

THE PHILOSOPHER'S DEATH

First of all, in terms of any living being, death appears as the abstract opposite of life. Every life is limited by its birth and death, which are understood as its limits: one as the moment at which life begins, the other as that in which it ends. In the case of the human being, however, unlike any other living being, the opposition between life and death is not merely an abstract one, but something *concrete*. In other words, the human being knows about its death and this knowledge has a concrete impact on its life. Philosophers have always argued that there is an essential relation between life, consciousness, truth and death. The Greek philosopher Plato (427–347 BC) defined life as the existence of the incarnate soul on earth. Life he understood as the ephemeral realm of appearances, while death is thought as the realm of the immutable, that is to say, of the never changing essence of things. In the world of appearances everything continually changes, therefore nothing is ever what it seems to be, while death is the dominion of truth, since here everything remains forever the same. On the one hand, we can see this already in the fact that we think of any true sentence as being true independently of time. On the other hand, this idea has been taken up in Christianity and in many other religions, where the idea of truth is related to the divine, and consequently understood as immortal, while a 'direct contact' with truth is for the human being tantamount to death. Consequently Plato argued that the specificity of the human being is given in that it is half animal and half god, where the latter part derives from its conscious relation to death as that which bestows truth to its knowledge.

Plato describes in one of his dialogues what such a consciousness of one's own death might mean. This dialogue, called *Phaedo*, is set on the day in which his teacher, Socrates, is going to drink poison following his death sentence on charges of corrupting the youth of Athens. Socrates speaks to his closest friends about the relation that the philosopher entertains with death. He argues that studying philosophy means to study dying and being dead. Other people might not understand this point, he explains, but that is because they are generally ignorant of the significance of the idea of death. They cannot understand the relation of philosophy to death, because they only know the abstract idea of death supervening at the end of life. They only know animal death and, this is Socrates' argument, as long as they do not understand this point, they will remain attached to animal life, barred from fulfilling their potential as human beings.

What then is this other death, the death the philosopher seeks? The truth of philosophy, Plato argues, is to realize that a relation to death, even when looking at a chair or at the distant stars, marks every moment of our lives. It is this relation to death that first of all enables us to have a relation to things at all. Consequently the possibility of our world rests on the special relation that the human being entertains with its death. The argument is that in the world of perception everything is in a state of continuous change or flux, so that it would be impossible for *one distinct thing* to appear. Only because the human being carries in its soul an image of the individual thing as it exists unchanging and eternally identical to itself in the true world, which is the world that is only truly present after death and before birth, can it identify *one thing* in the world, by overlaying the fleeting image of a perception with the stable image of what Plato calls an idea or form. It is, in other words, this relation to death, by which we are able to place ourselves 'outside' of immediate life. In this way we are able to take an 'objective' and 'theoretical' stance towards the world. Our whole existence is characterized by an ability to surpass our immediate surroundings, an ability which the philosophers call transcendence. Transcendence denotes a 'stepping over' from one realm to the other. Any knowledge of the world depends on this ability to step over the limitations of immediate existence by way of their negation. It is therefore by way of consciousness itself that the human being 'steps over' the limits of the realm of life and reaches into the divine dominion of death. We can now begin to see why the death of the philosopher is not the same as death understood as a fact of nature, in as much as it describes a relation to truth that transcends life. In other words, it is not only that the human being can think about death, but rather that its whole existence, even its sensibility, is marked and characterized by its relation to death. The human being, then, knows about its death in contrast to the animal to which death merely happens. To say that 'the human being knows about its death' is here already to say that it knows anything at all only because it stands in such a special relation towards death. Or, as Blanchot says, 'death, thought, close to one another to the extent that thinking, we die, if, dying, we excuse ourselves from thinking: every thought would be mortal; each thought the last thought (SNB 7). This connection with death, therefore, determines the existence and the essence of knowledge.

We can find another example concerning the peculiarity of the human relation to death in the text *The Myth of Sisyphus* by the French philosopher and novelist Albert Camus (1913–60). In the *Infinite Conversation* Blanchot singles out this myth, as it is interpreted by Camus, as the paradigmatic case of a philosopher attempting to carry off the victory over death (IC 176–81). This myth relates how Sisyphus tricked the gods in order to win, in death, eternal life. Expecting that the gods will take him to the underworld, Sisyphus tells his wife Merope that, should he die, she is neither to bury nor to perform the rites of passage for him. Subsequently, the god of war, Ares, takes his life. On the arrival of Sisyphus in the underworld, Thanatos, the god of the dead, is so enraged that Merope has dared to ignore the natural rites of burial that he sends Sisyphus back to life in order to punish her. The plan therefore succeeds, since Sisyphus returns to his life, and, instead of punishing his wife, he ignores the claim of Thanatos on his life and remains in our world for many more years. Yet, the important point of the story unravels only with his final death. Returning to the underworld, Thanatos punishes him for his disobedience by having him roll a stone up a mountain. Each time he reaches the precipice, the stone rolls back and Sisyphus has to start again. This is his punishment, that he has to repeat for all eternity.

This task, however, in its utter futility, is nothing else than an image of life as a properly circumscribed task, which, like the daily tasks in life, has no meaning beyond itself and is therefore always repeated again. Like a child who learns English literature in order to become a teacher and teach English literature to a child who now learns English literature, so Sisyphus repeats his task over and over again. Indeed, while the gods think they have punished Sisyphus, by a strange misunderstanding, they have given him, in a literal sense, *eternal life*. Sisyphus has then tricked the gods again and Camus concludes from here that one must imagine him happy. What this myth exemplifies is the human relation to death. Sisyphus can gain life only by way of his relation to death. Even to choose life on earth in favour of an eternal true 'life' is only possible in respect to the knowledge that is opened up by our transcendence towards death. This relation to death is, then, not only something that we have to acknowledge in theory. We have actively to seek and develop this relation and in this sense can it be said that we have to learn to die.

To learn dying and being dead, therefore, means to seek the perfect life. It is for this reason that Blanchot discusses Rainer Maria Rilke's (1875–1926) novel *Malte Laurids Brigge* (1910), in which the main character declares that the less people wish to have their own, proper death, the less can they hope for having their own life (SL 123–4). It then becomes clear, and here Blanchot agrees with Plato's account, that one can avoid death only at the price of losing the true life (SL 101). That is to say, that as long as we do not make sense of the time that is given to us as one limited by our own death, we are existing in a mean- ingless coming and going of day after day, where our life cannot form itself into one whole and meaningful existence. It is this theme that Blanchot discusses at great length in *The Space of Literature* (1955), for this notion of authentic death has led the philosophers to a particular interpretation of life, centring around the power of a subject that is the master of himself. Yet it is precisely from such an understanding that Blanchot wishes to move away, as it results in the alienation of the human being from its world. This is because the ideal of mastery has led philosophy to seek for an explanation of the meaning of human life from out of the idea of a solitary subject guided by the power of reason, so much so that the world appeared as merely a reflection of the subject him- or herself. The world itself, nature, history and art, have consequently lost their importance, until, in the twentieth century and still today, they appear only to the extent that they can be manipulated and fashioned according to our plans. Literature, on the contrary, is not something that we can master, rather it has a strange power over us, a power that we have to discover again.

To understand how Blanchot's conception of death brings it under the strange power of literature, we have first to understand the exem- plary form of the philosophical account of the power of subjectivity found in the mastery of death, which means, that we have to turn to the philosophy of G. W. F. Hegel.

HEGEL: 'MAN, THE MASTER OF DEATH'

For Hegel, it is not just the immortal soul that inhabits the world of death, but consciousness itself wields the power of death. The mastery of death here becomes the very meaning of the human being. The main difference between the human being, defined essentially as conscious, and all other living beings on this earth, consists in the fact that for consciousness everything else exists, while, for itself, consciousness is nothing. In other words, while we can say of everything else that it is *something*, consciousness is quite literally *no-thing*. In order to say of something that it exists, you will always have to be able to say where and when it exists. Yet, if a doctor, for example, attempts to look in the brain for this strange internal world, in which we watch all things pass in front of us, all she can find are grey cells and an activity of electrons and chemicals. Even if you were to answer that consciousness exists in inner reflection, you would still have a problem, because consciousness can be present, even to itself, only through the experience of something (you are thinking about the tree outside your window, or a memory of happier times), but never directly by apprehending itself. Take, for example, this book you are now reading. It is what your consciousness contains now. And yet your consciousness, as opposed to its content, is precisely *not this book*. Yet it is not *not this book*, by being something else, rather it is only this: '*not this book*'. Consciousness, when looking for itself, always finds something else; it finds the tree, but it is *not the tree*; it looks at a cat, but it is *not the cat*; it might even contemplate its 'own' hand or the tip of 'its' nose, and yet, it is *not the hand* and *not the nose*. You can play this game to infinity, but the result remains that consciousness is always *not this* and *not that*. Hegel simply calls consciousness a *nothingness in general*, and as such it is inseparable from death.

We might understand this inseparability by saying that consciousness can only be through death. But to understand death here, we must distinguish between two kinds of death, which we have already met with in our discussion of Plato: death as the simple end of life, and death as an integral part of life expressing a disappearance that is also a process of gaining something new. Thus, while a storm might just wreck a tree, the human being makes of the disappearance of the tree the appearance of a table. We can only understand such a death through the power of negativity by means of which consciousness 'vanquishes' the destructive power of death. For it is the nothingness of conscious- ness that brings to presence the thing as an idea, the 'book,' the 'tree' and the 'cat' that we spoke of earlier (see p. 32). In consciousness, pure negativity is no longer mere destruction but a *creative* destruction. The true life of consciousness is thus not opposed to death, but lives and sustains itself in death. This is to say that consciousness does not suffer the lack or disappearance of something, of food, of love or of justice, for example, but that it is precisely this lack that brings consciousness alive as the force that brings an end to what is in order to create some- thing new. In other words, consciousness is only in the sense that it masters death and turns it from being something that happens to it into its own power. In this respect Hegel sees the history of mankind as the domination of the world by way of a systematic knowledge of the world based on the mastery of death.

Perhaps the highest symbol of consciousness's power over death is the act of suicide. Suicide designates the ability not only to negate objects around me, but also myself, and this act is the supreme act of my will. Here death is not the death of the animal, which can never decide to take its life, but the philosopher's death par excellence, since death has become an idea, a principle and a project. Blanchot dedicates a section of *The Space of Literature* to Arria, a Roman woman and wife of Caecina Poetus (SL 100–3). In this story Arria, when seeing her husband hesitating in the act of suicide, takes his dagger, stabs herself in the breast, draws the knife from her body, and offers it to her husband with the words 'See, it does no ill!' As Blanchot remarks, we admire in Arria her resolve and her mastery of life. We esteem the utter vibrancy of life in a person committing suicide in such an autonomous manner.

Blanchot's interest in this story is that it implies the same end as Hegel's philosophy, namely the mastery of death. The problem for Blanchot is that this mastery of death, the philosopher's death, also means a 'turning away' from the other kind of death. In reaching out for death, in making of death a decision, death escapes me. Instead of having achieved the highest point of my freedom, the power of grasping death in my own hands, I find myself stripped of all my powers. Those who believe themselves to have conquered death in suicide make of death an ideal, and have thereby not got any closer to its reality.

The idea of suicide is here that of a *logic of decision*, where the ideal of activity shows itself in the attempt to mark time by the incision of this moment sealing the meaning of life. It is hence opposed to the actual becoming of life, to the interminable flow of time that makes up the flow of our existence. Having fled this character of interminability by putting an end to her life, Arria has also fled the temporality of life itself.

> For this point of view, Arria's impassivity is no longer the sign of the preservation of her mastery, but the sign of an absence, of a hidden disappearance, the shadow of someone impersonal and neutral.
>
> (SL 102)

The paradox of suicide, for Blanchot, leads to the experience of another death: neither death as a natural event, nor the human death to which the philosopher aspires, but an anonymous, impersonal and neutral death, which Blanchot calls a *dying stronger than death*. In the attempt to achieve the highest authenticity through the act of suicide, I discover another death beyond my grasp. Can I experience my death? Can I speak of such an experience as a possibility?

In 'Literature and the Right to Death', Blanchot links the domination of consciousness over the world to the power of language. Language, as we saw in Chapter 2, signifies the object only through its annihilation, and thus carries death within it:

> When I say 'This woman,' real death has been announced and is already present in my language; my language means that this person, who is here right now, can be detached from herself, removed from her existence and her presence, and suddenly plunged into a nothingness in which there is no existence or presence; my language essentially signifies the possibility of this destruction; it is a constant, bold allusion to such an event.
>
> (WF 323)

Here we can begin to see why Blanchot might think that literature has another relation to death than the one expressed by philosophy. The difference lies in the way in which we understand language. In philosophy, the negativity of language is under the power of the self who utters the word, expressing what it means to say. In literature, the word exceeds the intentions of the self. It is, therefore, a disappearance of both the object referred to in language, and the self who speaks the word. This disappearance relates to the double absence of literature that we also discussed in Chapter 2, since the 'I' too is a concept. The written word thus harbours the abandonment of the subject. When Shakespeare, for example, wrote his plays, he knew already that once written and performed, these plays would bring about his own disappearance as the one who expresses his ideas in them. The one whom we call Shakespeare exists now as a reflection of these plays, and the characters in the plays do not take their existence from the author, but from out of the words written. If we understand this negativity of language in its connection to death, then, in the first instance, it seems as if the one who speaks puts death to work. In negating the reality of things I hold them under my power. In the second instance, however, death can no longer be said to be mine, for it brings about both the disappearance of the object and of myself.

This ambiguity of death, being the origin of my existence while also bringing about the demise of the self-sufficient subject of modern philosophy, has been explored in the most decisive terms by the philosopher Martin Heidegger in his book *Being and Time* (1927), which we shall now go on to discuss in more detail.

THE QUESTION OF DEATH IN HEIDEGGER'S *BEING AND TIME*

Let us trace the question of death in Heidegger's work. First of all the human being exists. The verb 'to exist' is used here in distinction to the word 'to be'. A stone, on the one hand, is this or that, and its being is exhausted by such descriptions. The human being, on the other hand, exists in the sense of 'being able to be'. We might say, preliminarily, that it has a choice in the sense that its existence is not once and for all fixed. This choice has something to do with knowledge. Only if I know what I am, what I want and what I can do, can I make a choice and attempt to make it a reality. Insofar as my life consists of these choices and what becomes of them, one might say that I am concerned about my being, while a stone, for example, is quite indifferent as to what it is.

What does it mean, however, to choose something? It means to consider it as a whole, to look at it from every perspective. Yet how can I look at my life as a whole, since it has not yet come to an end and is therefore still incomplete? Indeed, as long as I am alive, I *am* always something *not yet*. The difficulty, it seems, is that one could only really know one's own life after death, for then it has run its course. But evidently this knowledge is not something open to me, since when it is available I will be dead. My life as a whole seems only to exist in the eyes of those that survive me. Only they will be able to judge whether my life has been truly worth living or not. As long as I am alive I cannot know myself and when I am dead, *I* will not know myself either. To close this gap we have got used to understanding our life from the viewpoint of others, and it is for this reason that we understand death as well as something that happens to others, which is to say to 'everybody'. Consequently we have become habituated to mistake death for an abstract fact of life.

This way of looking at oneself from the viewpoint of others, Heidegger argues, fails to understand existence as one's own. Here one generally considers one's existence as merely one example amongst many of a human life, just as one says that one table is just as much like another. Yet, for Heidegger, what belongs essentially to human existence, as opposed to any other kind of being, is that it has the possibility of being genuinely *singular*. On the whole, as Heidegger is well aware, we do not live individual lives, but merely follow the fashion of everyone else. We wear the same clothes, watch the same TV programmes, read the same books and even hold the same opinions as everyone else. Such a way of living describes our general mode of existence. Heidegger calls it inauthentic, but without implying moral censure. There is, however, for Heidegger, the possibility of authentic existence, and the clue to its possibility is the relation between death and time.

How does my life become something that I choose rather than something that others choose for me? We have said that insofar as our lives are determined through the future as the place of our hopes, plans and projections, we are always something not yet. The whole of my life is then never anything already given, but constitutes the meaning of my future. But this future of myself, even though essentially belonging to myself, is not something within my control. Rather it announces itself as anguish, as the insecurity of what I will be able to achieve and what fate has in store for me. And yet it is only in surpassing my present life towards this future fulfilment that I can relate to my existence as a whole. This whole is, then, not the totality of all attributes of myself, but rather the free projection of myself towards my future possibilities stretching towards 'my nothingness', that is, my death. In order to exist authentically I then have to understand that I am an essentially temporal being, and that the time characterizing my existence cannot be understood in the abstract and theoretical sense of time that we measure in seconds, minutes and hours, but has to be understood in its concrete temporal span. Yet, the concrete time of any one human being is the time that is given between its birth and its death. Thus, for you and I, unlike the stone, the past is never just something past, nor the future simply something that is not yet; rather past and future are integral parts of our present lives. While my past is what I am, the future, in terms of my expectations and hopes, determines my very existence in the present. The temporality of existence is, therefore, not the *abstract* temporality of the time-line, but the *concrete* temporality of life where the present arrives from the future while resting on the past.

What is our relation to death? It is either a fearful and passive waiting for the last moment to come, which paralyses us, because it seems to bring our lives to an end. Or, as Heidegger insists, it can become a question of an active anticipation of death as the ultimate horizon in which one chooses one's existence. Yet even for Heidegger death is the strangest possibility of all. It is, he says, the *possibility of impossibility*; that is to say, the possibility that all our possibilities come to an end. Such a possibility reveals to us that our existence is not like that of a stone lasting forever. If it were not for the presence of death, we would remain in the illusion that things could just go on as they are and therefore we would not have to do anything about our lives. The relation to death, then, determines the duality of human life between actuality and possibility. First of all, only a being that entertains such a relation to death can have possibilities, and, second, with death itself appears this rather strange possibility of our life, namely that all my possibilities come to an end, so that I turn back into a thing, the dead body. We see then that the limit of our possibilities, namely death, is also their source.

Death for Heidegger, as the most extreme possibility, reveals to us the impermanence and fragility of human existence, which means that our lives are a task and struggle, for at any moment we know that all we have achieved could disappear. Moreover, for Heidegger it is only death that truly makes me unique. In everything else that I am I can be substituted by another. I can say that 'I *am* a teacher' or 'I *am* a milkman' or even 'I *am* the lover of X', but at certain moments in my life I have to realize painfully that in all these positions I can be replaced. Somebody else could become the teacher, the milkman or even the lover. Yet there is one possibility in which I cannot be replaced and that is in my death. We can begin to see why, therefore, it is only with *my* death that I can begin to grasp *my* existence as a whole; that is to say, that *my* existence becomes a question for me. For only in relation to my death am I truly individualized. Indeed, considering the essential role that death plays in our life, Heidegger defines life as an interminable dying.

Blanchot will not so much disagree with this existential description of death, but argue that it is only one side of what he calls the two sides of death. The philosophical notion of death, then, hides behind its persuasiveness another more essential death, which is not the ground of my own authentic existence, but rather, as we shall see in Blanchot's discussion of politics, that of a community existing only in its dispersion. Blanchot calls this other death the *impossibility of possibility*, insofar as here I become aware of the illusion essential to all possibility. This 'other death' will be the topic of the next chapter, and we will show how it is linked to the question of literature.

EXISTENTIALISM

A philosophical movement stretching from the nineteenth-century philosophers Søren Kierkegaard (1813–55) and Friedrich Nietzsche (1844–1900) to the twentieth century in the work of Martin Heidegger (1889–1976), Gabriel Marcel (1889–1973), Jean-Paul Sartre (1905–80) and Maurice Merleau-Ponty (1908–61). All these authors stress the specific nature of human existence, which they understand as essentially free. In opposition to a long history of moral thought, which had proceeded by asking what the human being is, in order to derive from an answer to this question what it should do, the existentialist argues that the human being is first of all nothing. Existentialism, consequently, gives particular importance to the philosophy of action, arguing that human reality cannot be explained by science, since it is not concerned with facts. There are no strictly defined facts fashioning my existence, which is why Sartre argues that we are condemned to freedom, because we cannot escape the demand to turn the nothingness of our existence into a meaningful life by means of our actions.

SUMMARY

The idea of death has always been a central and defining feature of Western philosophy. Rather than escaping the anguish of death, philosophers have argued that only on account of our relation to death can a fulfilled life be won. This is not least because the idea of truth, without which we would not have any meaningful knowledge, is essentially related to the idea of death. Knowledge is only of worth if it holds true over time, and while both truth and death are thought as free of change, life appears as the realm in which everything is in constant change, so that nothing can ever hold true without being linked to death. This link is even stronger in the case of our own death, because only with death does our life become a meaningful whole.

In the nineteenth century, Hegel grasped death as the ultimate power of consciousness, through the mastery of which the human being becomes a fully rational being taking its fate into its own hands. Here the idea of negation, that is to say, of all change, of that which is possible or in the process of becoming, is understood as the power of the human subject. In Hegel's thought the philosophical notion of death finds its clearest expression, and it is, then, not surprising that the centrepiece of his system is the idea that consciousness lives and sustains itself by way of appropriating death as its most proper possibility. With this thought the human being is understood as the sheer activity of labour in the face of a passive world. Yet here already, we can see that our mastery of death derives from the negation inherent in language, because consciousness is first of all the power of language.

In the first part of the twentieth century, Heidegger began to argue that such an idealization of death is not much different from the ignorance of death, which philosophy had originally decried. This is because both the ignorance of death as well as its idealization make of death something which has no power over us. Instead, Heidegger argues, death has to be understood as that which fundamentally limits our knowledge and puts into question our understanding of the human being as self-present, rational and self-conscious. Such a death Heidegger calls 'the possibility of impossibility', that is to say, the possibility that all our life and its plans could at any moment, unforeseen and uncontrolled, be brought to naught. From out of this realization of its being-towards-death the human being can achieve an authentic life, which is to say, a life that is properly its own. It is from this position of philosophical thought, seeking in death the fulfilment of life, that Blanchot will begin his critique. and describe the reality of an anonymous, impersonal and neutral experience of a dying stronger than death. Such an experience will show itself alongside the experience of literature.

4

DEATH

From philosophy to literature

In this chapter we will investigate Blanchot's critique of the philosophical notion of death. Blanchot argues that such an investigation is necessary not only to find an answer to a philosophical question, but also in order to approach literature. This is why death plays such a central role in his meditation on literature, as one can see in some of the early essays like 'Literature and the Right to Death' (1948, WF 300–44), 'The Work and Death's Space' (1955, SL 85–159) or 'Literature and the Original Experience' (1952, SL 209–47), as well as in his later work, as, for example, in *The Infinite Conversation* (1969). The question of death concerns not only the end point of life, but the very meaning of writing. It is in relation to death that we first of all experience a feeling of dread, which relates us to a nothingness at the heart of our existence. And it is this experience, Blanchot argues, that gives rise to the demand of writing.

In the last chapter we have shown that the thought of death has been central to all Western philosophy. What Blanchot criticizes in respect to this tradition is that it reduces death to its 'positive' side, that is to say, to the activity and knowledge that arises from it. This desire of overcoming the dread of death is expressed in the dream of writing the definitive book, the most outstanding novel, which might bestow immortality on its author. But death cannot be overcome and the book, once written, always disappears in the face of the demand of the work which made the author write it. This is to say, the book always and necessarily falls short of what it tried to achieve and remains only as a hint towards a work that will never be accomplished. The author never experiences the fulfilment of a book well done and finished. As far as writing is a response to this nothingness of existence, every book signifies for the author the distance that separates him or her from 'his or her work'. The philosophers, Blanchot will argue, cannot really understand death, because it shows itself only in the experience of literature. Literature and death are then united in what, Blanchot argues, is an original experience of life. This experience only becomes intelligible on account of what he calls the two sides of death.

DYING AND DEATH

And yet, Blanchot's 'other' death is not directly opposed to the authentic death thought by the philosophers; rather it inhabits the extreme limit of life and death, a limit that is marked by his inversion of the Heideggerian phrase characterizing death as 'the possibility of impossibility' (see p. 47) to 'the impossibility of possibility'. Here death is not something that forces me authentically to grasp the significance of my life, rather it is something that wears me down. In Blanchot's fictional work, this other death is often conveyed by a long passage through a debilitating illness, where not even deliverance is promised, for one is forever dying but not dead. Thus the narrator recounts the dying of J. in *Death Sentence*:

> I arranged things with the nurse so that I could return to the hotel, where I stayed about an hour, and when I came back, Louise told me that she was still the same. But I saw right away that her condition had changed a good deal: the death rattle had begun and her face was the face of a dying person; besides that, her mouth was almost open which had never happened to her at any time before, while she was sleeping, and that mouth open to the noise of the agony, did not seem to belong to her, it seemed to be the mouth of someone I didn't know, someone irredeemably condemned, or even dead. ... The rattling became so loud and so intense that it could be heard outside the apartment with all the doors closed.

(DS 28–9)

This experience is that of the horror of the absence of the world, of an absence of meaning in which all my abilities become unreal, until 'I' myself disappear in the passivity of dying. In dying one is exposed to existence deprived of the world of action. In such existence the idea of authentic death, as the origin of my knowledge, is transformed into the infinite passivity of dying, where the one who dies encounters the impossibility of dying, that is to say, the impossibility of turning the world into something meaningful (WF 334). This impossibility Blanchot calls the space of non-origin, where we have lost the right to our own death. Instead of finding in death the ground of my individuality, that which is properly mine and in regard to which I cannot be replaced, 'my' death rather exposes me to the dissipation of myself, to the experience of an insufferable anonymity. In reality, Blanchot argues against Heidegger, 'I' never die, but 'one dies' (SL 241). The impossibility of dying, then, does not defy our understanding because of our ignorance, but leads to the idea of another thinking, that is not characterized by power, a thinking that no longer understands itself as the activity of negation. This is not to say that Blanchot disagrees with Heidegger's analysis of our repression of death by means of its abstraction, as when we think it a banality that 'everyone dies'. But dying is this movement where I can no longer push death away from me by attributing it to 'everyone'. Rather here I become 'everyone', that is, I lose myself and experience how 'one dies'.

Dying then reveals to me an anonymous and impersonal power separating me from myself. In other words, to encounter the impossibility of dying means to say that dying deprives me of the power to say 'I'. While the first side of death appears as the very power of knowledge, grasping even its own limit, the other side of death is already revealing, beneath the appearance of mastery, the horror of an existence deprived of the world. The experience of the impossibility of dying reveals the impossibility of understanding the world as my world through the act of my proper death. Being alive I might dream of a convenient death, bringing my life to a perfect end, but dying ruins the idea of death determined as activity (SL 103–4). Behind the hope invested in the thought that 'I' die and that my death will let my life shine in its perfection, lies the anguish of the 'one dies', of an indescribable horror of meaninglessness (SL 128). While I was looking for the moment that ends my life, this anonymous death that happens to me does not put an end to anything, but rather makes my life disappear into insignificance (WF 340). The time of dying is then no longer the idea of a future occupied with ideas of my authentic self-fulfilment, but is determined through suffering as the presence that does not pass away, while being nothing but the experience of an indiscriminate passing, where time flows without past or future. Insofar as this passivity is no longer even a stance that I can take voluntarily, Blanchot calls it, following Emmanuel Levinas, a passivity more passive than all passivity.

Such a description of dying seems to have nothing in common with the philosophical conception of death as we described it in the last chapter. While the *interminability of dying* determined Heidegger's discourse as much as Blanchot's, they seem to speak about different experiences: Heidegger about the life stretching out towards my death, Blanchot about the experience of dying permeating life. Indeed, it looks as if the philosophical account of death does not leave any space for the experience of dying. In this life, I have a relation to my own death, a death that determines my future and which might arrive at any time, and, while this realization affects the way I choose to live my life, it still consists of a refusal of the actual meaninglessness of dying.

ONTOLOGY

Ontology is the science of being (from the Greek *on, ontos*, Being; and *logos*, the word, reason or science). Ontology is that part of philosophy that attempts to discover the essential features of everything that exists, independent from actual experience. Ontology thus comprises the doctrine of being as such, the most universal concepts of being and their meaning. If Aristotle, for example, devises a table of categories, then these are descriptions of any being as such, that is, characteristics that any actual thing has to have. Examples of such categories are substance, quantity, quality, time or location.

If philosophy is involved in the attempt to vanquish death, then this happens by separating the ontological value of death from the (un)reality of dying itself. The temptation of the eternal, expressed in such rejection of death, leads us to the edification of the world of understanding, behind which 'the truth' of 'universal corruption' is forgotten (IC 33). In other words, we tend to deny death in order not only to dream of our own immortality, but also because this immortality persuades us that the world itself will always remain the same.

This was why Hegel needed the conception of a death stronger than dying, enabling him to *separate the world from its other, by separating death from dying*. One might say that the refusal of death lies at the origin of a philosophy that ends up reducing the world and our existence to knowledge. Thus the philosophical conception of death leads to a reduction and alienation of our life.

With the thought of the interminability of dying, Blanchot seeks to redress the intellectualism of a modernity that understands negation as purely logical, constructing the world itself as something that I can understand in its totality. To understand negation as purely logical is to say that the world itself is taken merely 'to be there', while all change and development is due to human activity, whether by thought or labour. It is in this respect that Blanchot's thinking appears, first of all, to be directed against what is accepted to be the major aim of philosophy, namely to further the activity of the human being. Such furtherance of human activity demands that whatever happens can be understood as deriving from human action, so that everything that is appears as 'my deed'. Here the world is purely passive, while the human being is the pure force of negation, that is of action in the world. On the contrary, Blanchot searches for a passivity in us, which would allow us to be responsive to what is other than knowledge. Yet this responsiveness is always already closed down, as soon as we attempt to find in death our highest possibility.

Death is the limit of life. Literature, or, as Blanchot comes to call it, writing, harbours an experience of that which precedes life. This is because, while I can possibly think of spoken language as an expression of an idea the speaker has at the moment, writing makes the historical nature of language apparent. One might say that writing is used to preserve such ideas for the future, and hence we can still read Shakespeare today, even though he certainly has no longer any ideas in mind. But it is also the case that writing makes us aware of the historical depth of language, that is, of the fact that when I read or write, the language that I encounter expresses a world before my birth and, indeed, a world even independent of the author. We thus encounter in literature a language that does not depend on anyone, that does not find its meaning in the mind of any human being. But that is to say that literature cannot be reduced to the deed of an author, that it resists the intellectualism we discussed in the last paragraph. We are then looking in literature for an original experience complicit with death. As

Blanchot says, literature has made a pact with death, it is itself an experience of death, of an extreme passivity. Such an experience is difficult to describe, and we wonder how an expression like 'the impossibility of possibility' could enlighten us. While this appears, at first, as a mere game with words, turning around Heidegger's formulation of 'death as the possibility of impossibility' (see p. 47), understood against the background of modern philosophy it makes a lot of sense, considering that we have determined possibility in relation to our activity, itself essentially understood as negation and thus as labour transforming the world. This was what was meant by saying that modern philosophy understands negation as purely logical: that the world is what it is and that everything that is not yet but is possible can become actual only by means of human action. Here we can follow a clue of language: the word 'possibility' derives from the Latin verb '*posse*', which translates as 'to be able to'. But any ability presupposes a knowing, which is in turn an appropriation of the known, and, as appropriation, a form of violence, turning what is into that which is known. In other words, while philosophy suffers from an ignorance of dying, as soon as I attempt to conceptualize dying, I immediately fall back into the concept of death as an appropriation of the world, understanding it as that which I have accomplished myself.

> Do we approach the anonymous if we yield (supposing that there were enough passivity in us for such a concession) to the attraction of dying, indeed, of thought? If to think were to sink into nothingness, as we would think with happiness, with fright. But, sinking through thought, we are immediately carried to our highest possible.
>
> (SNB 38)

SINGULARITY: THE SECRET OF BEING

We will next see how Blanchot's later philosophy develops his reflection on death by enriching it with the notions of passivity and the other. If, in his earlier work, Blanchot talks about death in terms of negativity and absence, in his later work, beginning with the *Infinite Conversation* (1969), he will increasingly focus on the relation between death and the other. These two themes are not opposed to one another, for, as we have already seen, everyday language negates the particular thing in favour of the universal communicability of the concept. As all my relations with the world are mediated by language, it seems I cannot understand the world of singular beings. From here derives the ambiguity of the word 'other', which is, on the one hand, that which is other than the world of knowledge, and on the other, more specifically, the other human being, who, as a singular being, belongs as well to the ineffable. One might then say that singularity is the secret of being, and it is this secret that is approached by literature and the experience of dying.

Why should there be anything wrong about feeling at home in a world that appears to be the result of our own activity? If philosophy originates in the refusal of facing the reality of dying then it seems that there is 'something' before the world of knowledge, something that seems incomprehensible to philosophy but given as an experience of literature, of a literature that constantly questions the essence of things before the world comes to be. This brute and material origin of the world, according to Blanchot, is essentially experienced in the way that literature deals with the materiality of the word, as discussed in Chapter 2. Having shown that the philosophical concept of death is incomplete, Blanchot can demonstrate that philosophy is not an independent and hence self-sufficient thinking, since it is dependent on that which forever escapes its grasp. This 'something' would be the 'immediate' thing before the act of knowing apprehension. Here we would be privy to the presence of what is other than the familiar objects of our world precisely insofar as it differs from them. We have argued above, that the normal use of language negates the singular thing in order to be able to speak it. What we are thus speaking about is, first of all a universal, and it has become so by the mediation of language. Speaking about a friend, for example, we realize that the language we use automatically turns him or her into something abstract, into a man or woman, with these or those characteristics. We attempt to communicate what is particular about him or her, but all we can do is add more and more general qualities or abstract events, like birth dates or names. We feel that we are doing her or him injustice, that all that is left to us is to refuse to speak about him or her. The singular being, that which refuses mediation, is then, by necessity, that which is given, if at all, in an immediate way. This is why Blanchot calls such immediate singularity the secret of being, insofar as it cannot be expressed in everyday language. But everyday language still depends on this existence of its other and a complete separation from this secret would make our communication completely meaningless. Human life cannot exist without this enigma and can then never strive towards a total understanding of the world. In this respect, Blanchot can say that 'the drawing back before what dies is a retreat before reality' (IC 34).

Here again, Blanchot claims that the promise of literature questioning philosophy consists in an overcoming of the alienation of our lives. Blanchot's redress for this alienation finds expression in his claim that:

> the important point is that the same effort has to be carried out with respect to literature as Marx carried out with respect to society. Literature is alienated, and is so in part because the society to which it is related is founded on the alienation of humanity.
>
> (BR 150)

But such overcoming is possible only if we can show that literature allows precisely that: a relation to the enigma of our singular existence, of an existence that cannot be said without being turned into something universal. The promise of literature thus does not consist in broadening our knowledge and in contributing to our mastery over the world but, on the contrary, in counteracting the alienation of human existence in a world of utility.

By the time of *The Infinite Conversation* (1969) and *The Unavowable Community* (1983), Blanchot's distancing from Heidegger has found its most radical formulation. Heidegger, as we have seen in the last chapter, related death exclusively to my own death, while Blanchot argues that death is never my own, and that I am only concerned with the death of the other (UC 21). This is a radical claim to make, because, as we have seen, Blanchot does not contradict Heidegger's critique according to which we generally view death as an abstract fact that happens to 'everyone'. Rather, death as breaching my individuality, death as the passivity that gives rise to the presence of the other, also gives rise to the community of human beings dispersed into singular beings still dependent on each other. In opposition to Heidegger, Blanchot therefore claims that the true experience of death entails that death is not a solitary event (UC 22). This idea of death, as we will see in later chapters, will be the source of Blanchot's political thought.

Blanchot, thinking through the idea of poetry, was influenced particularly by his reading of Heidegger's lectures on the German poet

Friedrich Hölderlin (1770–1843). In these lectures Heidegger argued that the origin of language cannot be sought in the negativity of the concept, which is to say, in the useful language of information, but is to be found in the inexpressible singularity of the name. The language proper to the singularity of the name is poetry and in poetry, then, lies the origin of all language. It sometimes strikes us as uncanny when it is said that the poet names things. Naming seems to be something that we learned very early on in childhood. But here we have learned how people generally refer to classes of things, like all cups or all cats, while the naming of poetry attempts to say this one thing in its singular existence. When a poet names, for example, 'the horse', this is not to describe what horses are in general and to allow us to gain knowledge about them, but to say this one horse, that no longer exists and, indeed, that never really existed as an object of knowledge. Here there is no sense in asking if the poetic description of the horse is accurate, if it fits the horse in question. But why should we listen to a saying of something that is not there and that we have never seen nor are able to see? The tension in poetry is that it tries to bring something to language which cannot be said. Literature, in this understanding, does not engage in the furtherance of life, but is the quest for the origin of language. Literature does not then consist of descriptions of imaginary events and plots, but is:

> the eternal torment of our language, when its longing turns back toward what it always misses, through the necessity under which it labours of being a lack of what it would say.
>
> (IC 36)

Literature is not the imaginative and free invention of possible worlds, as it might appear if we have a look at novels that are conceived merely as the opportunity to idle away some spare time. Rather the essential question of all literature is: 'How can I, in my speech, recapture this prior presence that I must exclude in order to speak, in order to speak it?' (IC 36).

What is dying? The limit of this world and the passage into the other of the world. But this is also the idea of language in literature, giving rise to the world at the same time that it makes its reality unapproachable. This other death is also found within language, where the meaning of words is not determined by their information content, where language arises from the silent origin of word and thing, before being raised to the luminousness of the concept.

> [Literature] is not beyond the world, but neither is it the world itself: it is the presence of things before the *world* exists, their perseverance after the world has disappeared, the stubbornness of what remains when everything vanishes and the dumbfoundedness of what appears when nothing exists.
>
> (WF 328)

Generally we tend to presume that what lies before the expression of language is nothing but the things themselves, untouched and self-sufficient. To speak about the silence of this world, then, sounds like an appeal to the commonsense conviction of a world given independently from our existence as well as from language. But, as we have argued above, that there are distinct things is possible only through language as a power of negation. That there is 'a cat', for example, here in front of me is possible only by means of our ability to negate a singular thing in order to make 'a cat' out of it. That is to say that the existence of the cat depends on the ability of naming it and such everyday ability is originally dependent on the poetic word. But what is there before the negating labour of language, before the activity of the human being? For the above reasons we are here not looking for a world without language, but for the silence of language as it is expressed in literature.

THE ANONYMITY OF WRITING AND DEATH

For Blanchot, and for many of his contemporaries in France, modern philosophy since Hegel can be summed up as a philosophy of finitude; that is to say, the thinking of human beings facing up to the inevitability of their death in a world without God. At this moment in our history, death takes on a new meaning. This change of the meaning of death is of such a significance that it constitutes a radical change of our existence. Thus Blanchot often speaks of a time of transition, not due to specific historical events, but on the grounds of this great change in the human condition, deprived of the infinite meaning bestowed by God.

In the philosophical interpretation of death, absence is something useful. Such active relation to death allows me to refer to things even when they are absent, it measures the distance between the human being and any other living being and it is the very mark of my freedom.

In the case of language, the absence of the thing, its death, is also useful, for in this absence the concept rises up to fill the void. The sting of death is conquered and transformed into something positive. But we have already seen that, for Blanchot, the language of literature refers to a double absence: an absence not only of the thing but also of the concept. At this moment, absence is no longer useful, for the word can no longer be subsumed under the theoretical or practical activity of human reason.

On the one hand, this is literature's frivolousness, for it is not concerned with the reality of things, but with the beauty of the word. Yet, on the other hand, it reveals literature's connection to the strange and unsettling power of language. For what this absence points to is language's own reality, exceeding the power of consciousness to refer to things. When I name something, the word simply designates the object that has disappeared, but in literature this naming undergoes a strange transformation. It seems to turn in on itself, so that language no longer describes fictional realities but its own power of naming. When, as in the example above, a poet names 'a horse', he does not aim at evoking the image of a horse in our minds. His aim is not to make the words disappear behind the successful communication of the image. Rather, the more successful the poem, the more powerfully do the words stand in front of us and sound in our ears, and not the horse. Even though we have a tendency to think that literature constitutes merely a secondary use of language, the primary purpose of which is to refer to the reality of the world, Blanchot argues that the very uselessness of literature points toward the true origin of language. Language inscribes the distance that separates us from the reality of the world. Rather than being a mirror of what is real, language prevents us from accessing the real understood as independent. Indeed it is only in our everyday use of language and its modulation in higher forms of reasoning, like science, that we adhere to the belief that language represents the real world, whereas the study of literature reminds us that reality is an illusion that words make possible only by forever also banishing us from this reality.

If language does not merely concern the expression of thoughts that arise inside my head, then what is said by language exists entirely separate from my own, individual existence. It is not only the things that are annihilated by a language of which I make use, but 'I' myself disappear in it. On the one hand, this can be interpreted positively, and it has sometimes been the defence of literature: we write so that our words outlive us, so that in the eternal presence of a work we might be granted immortality. But this 'outliving us' has a more sinister and dark meaning. The words outlive me, because in a certain sense *my* existence is irrelevant to them.

This is how Blanchot's critical work connects to the celebrated thesis of the 'death of the author', a concept brought explicitly into existence by Roland Barthes (1915–80), a contemporary theorist of literature who both influenced and was influenced by Blanchot. This development has then led to the liberation of literary criticism from the shackles of the 'intentions of the author', which were never really available, were thus often only a means to assert one's own opinions, and which have always raised the question why we should turn to literature, if this only conveyed to us what an author could have said in a more factual manner. This independence of the text from the original author's intentions already marks their own absence from the scene of writing. Such absence marks the very demand of writing. This is why Blanchot can say that, in the end, it is death that speaks through me.

Like death, the demand of writing cannot be understood in terms of one of my possibilities. There is something faintly absurd, for Blanchot, in saying 'I am a writer', for writing is the very disappearance of the power of the self to say 'I'. That we can say 'I am a writer' is possible only because we can always emerge from the demand of the work into the light of the day, where writing is simply one activity amongst others. But the demand of writing is not the same as the activity of writing. The demand of writing emerges within the activity of writing and ruins it. This is why many writers' journals, of which Kafka's diaries are perhaps the prime example, are full of stories abortively begun. It also accounts for the strange quality of the modern novel, which, perhaps unlike its predecessors, is written under the hopeless search for a pure language that would respond to the demand of writing.

> To write without 'writing', to bring literature to that point of absence where it disappears, where we no longer have to fear its secrets which are lies, that is 'writing degree zero', the neutrality which every writer deliberately or unwittingly seeks, and which leads some to silence.
>
> (BR 147–8)

By the time of *The Space of Literature* (1955), Blanchot's approach to discussing the relation between literature and death, as we have already described, changes from the language of negativity, associated with Hegel, to Heidegger's language of possibility. Here what is underlined is not so much the violence of language, but the impossibility of conceiving of the demand of writing as an activity like any other. Blanchot here draws an analogy between the two sides of death, that he uncovered in his analysis of the paradox of suicide, and the two attitudes an author might take toward his or her own writing (SL 106). In analogy to the first side of death, signifying the meaningful negation of reality, there is literature as a cultural object, which we call the 'book'. This bears the author's name, is reviewed in newspapers, wins prizes and is the object serving literary critics to develop their ever new and resourceful theories. Both author and critic are here understood as actively in command of their skills. The other side of literature, analogous to the second side of death, Blanchot calls the 'work'. This work does not bear the name of the writer, is not spoken about in reviews, not taken into account when conferring literary prizes and resists any literary theory. It is the work that makes demands on the author, in the face of which she or he remains passive even and especially when trying to bring it into reality by writing a book. It is precisely on account of the work being concealed behind the objectivity of the book that we habitually confuse it with the latter, though we often feel, quite rightfully, that the culture industry that deals with and in books, is far removed from the experience of literature.

Why is it that the work, unlike the book, escapes the writer's name? At this point we are again thrown back on to Blanchot's conception of language. Just as much as language destroys the reality of the thing, it also consumes the individuality of the writer. The words written on the page seem to come from nowhere and no one. The 'I' of the writer is desubjectivized in the work, just as the resolute, courageous and authentic 'I' disappears in the 'other' death. But what do we mean by the impersonality of language and the anonymity of the author? It means that language should not be interpreted, as is mostly the case in linguistics, from the viewpoint of the subject of enunciation; that is, from the position of the 'I' that speaks. The language of the poem has an autonomy and distance from both the reader and the writer. It speaks for itself. This 'I' that speaks is invaded from within and without by this impersonal language so that what speaks in me is always more than me. In our everyday lives we repress or deny this. We simply get on with living. But the writer must advance into this impersonal language and allow it to speak in her place. This is what it means to be a writer, and why writing is not like any other activity.

Blanchot describes this annihilation of the author in the demand of writing through the ancient Greek myth of Orpheus who descends into Hades in order to bring his wife Eurydice back to life. Orpheus's music so moves Hades, the god of the underworld, that he allows Orpheus to return with his wife to the world of the living, but only on condition that, as they make their way back, he does not turn to look at her. They have almost completed their ascent when Orpheus, filled with anxiety, looks back to see if she is still behind him, thus breaking his promise, and she vanishes forever into the underworld.

On the surface, Blanchot remarks, it seems that the Greek myth concerns the punishment of Orpheus for his impatience. We should not forget, however, that Orpheus is a poet, and he is thereby already intimately acquainted with death. In the poems that he writes about Eurydice she is already absent. And to be a poet is to be already fascinated by the absence that words make possible. The love of Orpheus, even before he descended into the underworld, had already been characterized by her absence. His glance backwards is then merely a confirmation of this point. But in this glance she disappears and so the word never finds security in what we hope to represent. While, on the first side of death, we might hope to have overcome the fear of loss by way of an immortal work of art, the second side immediately appears, making us understand that the work has only intensified and realized the loss, the anguish of which has driven us to art.

> Through Orpheus we are reminded that speaking poetically and disappearing belong to the profundity of a single movement, that he who sings must jeopardize himself entirely and, in the end, perish, for he speaks only when the anticipated approach toward death, the premature separation, the adieu given in advance obliterate in him the false certitude of being, dissipate protective safeguards, deliver him to a limitless insecurity.
>
> (SL 156)

Such failure is not something that simply happens when one writes; it essentially belongs to all writing. At the end of the Greek myth, which is sometimes forgotten in its retelling, Orpheus's body is torn into pieces and thrown into a river. As the dismembered head floats down the river, it still sings of Eurydice. Literature is a language that no longer sounds on the lips of the living.

SUMMARY

In this chapter we have developed Blanchot's criticism of the philosophical account of death. While the latter characterizes death as the chance of the human being to determine its own life, Blanchot argues that the reality of death exposes me to an anonymous and impersonal power that separates me from myself and leaves me powerless. Instead of finding the meaning of our lives in a perfect end, the experience of dying is that of an indescribable horror of meaninglessness. And yet, Blanchot can only account for such a reality of death by criticizing the philosophical account, because he does agree that in the experience of death we are looking to overcome the alienation of human existence. The difference lies in that Blanchot claims that this alienation from the reality of the world is a result of the philosophical notion of death as enabling and empowering life. The more we become the active part in our relation to the world that surrounds us, the less significance the latter has. At the same time the active life of man loses any meaning. It is for this reason that Blanchot speaks of two sides of death. While on the one side we find our lives full of possibility, the other side exposes us to a passivity in the face of which all our possibilities turn into naught. Thus Blanchot opposes to Heidegger's idea of death as the possibility of impossibility the reality of death as the impossibility of possibility, which is an experience of a weakness in the face of an overpowering world.

This account of death opens the path to an experience of the reality underlying the world of action, which Blanchot names the secret of being: singularity. Whatever we talk about is by means of words turned into something universal. It is, for example, green, round or nasty, but these are all attributes that hold for many things. By contrast, that which makes a person this singular person is not sayable, which is why Blanchot calls it a secret. Here Blanchot links the thought of death to that of literature, because it is only in literature, and especially in poetry, that we leave the realm of knowledge and information in order to turn to the existence of the singular thing. Literature is, then, the quest for the origin of language.

This mutual implication of the thought of death and literature opens the way to understanding how they both are related to the experience of the other. It is first in the passivity opened up by the second side of death that I can experience something other to me, insofar as to be passive means to be receptive. The experience of death and literature, then, shows itself as the origin of the community of singular human beings. In stark contrast to Heidegger, Blanchot understands death not as the event that individualizes me in that it is solely my death with which I am concerned. Rather death exposes me to the anonymity of an interminable dying.

In the experience of literature, we realized that there are two sides to the thought of death. We can explicate this ambiguity by the difference that Blanchot expounds between the book and the work. While the first side is given in the form of the author presenting a book as his or her work, thus celebrating his or her activity and being praised for his or her skill, the reality of writing, according to Blanchot, is reached only by that which he calls the work. The work is what first of all made the author write a book. Here already the author responded to a demand of writing rather than deciding what to do. The book has any reality only by fulfilling the claim of the work. Yet, as the work of literature refers to singularity as the secret of being, that is, to something that cannot be said, any book necessarily falls short of the demand of the work. What the first side of death made appear as a success, the second immediately translates into an experience of failure. Literature is, then, complicit with the experience of dying, and indeed, as Blanchot argues, the literary author dies in his or her work, insofar as the language he or she uses, instead of expressing his or her intentions, makes the authorial voice disappear behind the anonymous language of literature.

5

LITERATURE AND ETHICS

The impact of Levinas

In this chapter we shall begin to analyse a change in direction and style of Blanchot's work. The change in style marks an increasing blurring of the margins between Blanchot's critical and fictional work and we shall say more about this in the first section of this chapter. The change in direction is Blanchot's growing focus on ethical and political questions in relation to literature. It is this that will become the significant topic of the next chapters of the book. In this chapter we will concentrate on the importance of ethics in Blanchot's work. We shall see that for Blanchot this relation can only be thought through the ethics of Emmanuel Levinas. Before we go on to the portrayal of the influence of Levinas's ethics on Blanchot, however, we shall investigate the first point of contact between their work, which is the phenomenon of the 'there is'. Even though Levinas's ethics is an important factor in understanding Blanchot's work, we also want to show the important difference in how they conceive of the status of writing. This will enable us to introduce the important concept of the 'neuter' in Blanchot's work and give a fully rounded description of his concept of both language and literature.

BLANCHOT'S STYLE

Before publication of *The Infinite Conversation* (1969), we could speak of

Blanchot's work being divided into two parts: on the one side, there were his novels or narratives, and, on the other, his critical essays. Commencing with *The Infinite Conversation*, however, this distinction becomes increasingly blurred. Thus, the first pages of this book, which like Blanchot's other critical works would appear to be a collection of essays initially published in journals, begins with a description of a conversation between two exhausted interlocutors that might have been part of one of Blanchot's own novels or narratives (IC xiii–xxiii). The rest of the book is continually interrupted at decisive points by their conversations, though we are unsure whether they are the same two weary questioners. It is worth noting that the treatment of Levinas's philosophy is also staged in the form of a conversation, which undermines our own habit of ascribing positions and opinions portrayed in a work as being sustained by the authority of the author's voice. Is it Blanchot who speaks there, or someone else? To which of the voices, if any, would we attribute Blanchot's views? To quote from *The Infinite Conversation* only conceals this problem, for the quotations are taken out of the context of the conversation, and thereby presented as though the text spoke through a unitary voice. The principle of conversation already counteracts our desire for a single truth that would be the object of the agreement of all. There is no first or last word, only an infinite dialogue to which we all belong, but which none of us could be said to possess or direct.

Our confusion and bewilderment is only exacerbated by subsequent publications. On opening *The Step not Beyond* (1973) or *The Writing of Disaster* (1980), we might be excused for being unsure whether at one time we are reading a philosophical work, even though a very strange and fragmented one, and, at another time, something literary. Thus, in the middle of *The Writing of Disaster*, we read a description of what Blanchot calls a 'primitive scene' of a child staring out of a window at an absent sky, leaving us uncertain as to whether it is a part of a story or even a fragment of his own autobiography (WD 72). Likewise, on opening one of Blanchot's last narratives, *Awaiting Oblivion* (1962), which describes a conversation between a man and women about an event that is about to happen or that might already have happened, we may be unsure whether we are reading literature or philosophy, a confusion which is only increased once we have learned that part of this narrative was published in a collection of essays on the philosopher Martin Heidegger. It should not surprise us, therefore, that *The Infinite*

Conversation itself begins with the statement that the question of literature has rendered this distinction between a critical work and an artistic one useless, perhaps because in our own time every true artistic work is already critical of its own status as art:

> Certainly there are always books published in every country and in every language, some of which are taken as critical works or works of reflection, while others bear the title of novel, and others call themselves poems. ... Still, this remark must be made: since Mallarmé (reducing the latter to a name and the name to reference point), what has tended to render such distinctions sterile is that by way of them, and more important than they are, there has come to light the experience of something one continues to call, but with a renewed seriousness, and moreover in quotation marks, 'literature'.
>
> (IC xi)

None of this, however, should lead us to think that there are not substantial philosophical problems that Blanchot engages with in *The Infinite Conversation*. One of the most important of these problems is the relation between literature and ethics. This will be the topic of the next sections, and we shall see, just as with the relation between death and literature, where his interlocutor was Martin Heidegger, that Blanchot will engage with this problem through a dialogue with another thinker. In this case, the dialogue will be with Emmanuel Levinas.

THE IMPACT OF LEVINAS

Blanchot's intellectual biography is marked by strong friendships that have shaped the evolution of his own thought. The friendship between Blanchot and Levinas was marked by their continual engagement with each other's work. On Blanchot's side, Levinas introduced him to phenomenology and the philosophy of Martin Heidegger, but more importantly, perhaps, the effect of Levinas's writing was to keep the question of ethics open for Blanchot, when for most it had already become a closed issue.

PHENOMENOLOGY

Phenomenology is a method of philosophy initiated by the German philosopher Edmund Husserl (1859–1938) and is one of the most important schools of contemporary philosophy. It aims at a pure description of appearances as they are given by experience without recourse to any extraneous assumptions about the status of the existence of these appearances. Its famous slogan is 'back to the things themselves'. Thus, for example, Husserl, in his work *Ideas: A General Introduction to Pure Phenomenology* (1913) talks about his apple tree growing in his garden. His method is to describe this tree as it appears in perception without appealing to any external theory. It thus eschewed both metaphysics and the natural sciences as the method proper to philosophy. Phenomenology was quickly taken up in France both through the work of Edmund Husserl and his student Martin Heidegger who developed a more concrete phenomenology. Perhaps the most famous French phenomenologist was Jean-Paul Sartre (1905–80), and thus phenomenology was the basic precursor for twentieth-century existentialism. Blanchot gained his access to phenomenology through Emmanuel Levinas, who wrote one of the first and most important introductions to Edmund Husserl's work *The Theory of Intuition in Husserl's Phenomenology* (1930). Blanchot does not write directly on phenomenology, but there is some support for the view that his work of the 1950s, especially *The Space of Literature* (1955), is influenced by the phenomenological method in its return to the phenomenon itself (in this case literature) by bracketing any assumptions about the status of its existence.

For Blanchot, the experience of writing and the demand of ethics are inseparable. Such a statement seems flatly to contradict his literary theory that entails, as we showed in the previous chapters, the absolute autonomy of literature in relation to the world. Literature, Blanchot appears to argue, has its own truth, which lies outside justice. And yet this loyalty towards the purity of the literary work seems to contradict Blanchot's continued engagement in political causes throughout his life. Is it a matter, therefore, of splitting his life into two? On the one side, the private and solitary pursuit of his literary work, and, on the other, the public membership of political groups? This split would be the easiest solution, but, as we shall see, it is a gross oversimplification.

For this reason, the political groups to which he belonged, at least after the 1930s, were as secretive and guarded as his own persona as a writer and, more importantly, such a simple and transparent split contradicts the very indivisibility of writing and ethics that is at the heart of his critical practice. Perhaps the solution to this problem is not to be found in our understanding of Blanchot's life, but in our preconceptions about ethics and its distance from literary theory. We assert that there is a contradiction here because we are certain that literature and ethics are two quite separate spheres, or we simply reduce the content of literature to an ethics, and thus lose what is specific to literature. Blanchot's response might be that the labyrinthine relation between the demand of ethics and literature is far more complex than these hasty opinions assert, especially if we begin with Levinas's description of the relation to the other.

For Levinas, the demand of ethics is not to be understood in the defence of values, as it is conceived in moral philosophy. The demand of ethics, rather, is the exposure of the self to excessive presence of the other who calls into question my ownership of the world. The other, as Levinas would say, demands a response from me, an interruption of my selfishness, and this 'response' is the true impetus behind responsibility. The link between this and writing is that for Blanchot literature too is an exposure of the self to an excessive demand that calls into question the dominance of the subject. The position of the writer is quite different, for example, from the portrayal of the romantic solitary genius as someone who breaks the rules of artistic content and expression by the power of his creativity that shapes the recalcitrant artistic material to his will. To write is not to write from a position of authority, but in the absence of power. It is not an act of will or resolution, but extreme passivity, where the powers of the self are undone. Both ethics and literature are evidence of a 'human weakness' more primordial than the weakness of the will (WD 44).

In the following sections we will focus on the philosophy of Emmanuel Levinas, whose importance to Blanchot's own thought can be gathered from his forceful affirmation of the philosophical importance and originality of perhaps Levinas's most famous work *Totality and Infinity*:

> In Emmanuel Levinas's book – where, it seems to me, philosophy in our time has never spoken in a more sober manner, putting back into question, as we

must, our ways of thinking and even our facile reverence for ontology – we are called upon to become responsible for what philosophy essentially is, by entertaining precisely the idea of the Other in all its radiance and in the infinite exigency that are proper to it, that is to say, the relation with the [other]. It is as though, there were here a new departure in philosophy and a leap that it, and we ourselves, were urged to accomplish.

(IC 51–2)

Before we begin to question the meaning of the ethical relation and how it is linked to the question of writing and ethics, however, we shall need to make a detour to inquire into a phenomenon that first drew the work of Blanchot and Levinas together: the 'il y a' or the 'there is'.

THE *IL Y A*

Let us turn to a book by Levinas called *From Existence to Existents* (1947), which had a powerful influence on Blanchot's early work and has much in common with his early novels such as *Thomas the Obscure* (1941) and *The Most High* (1948). In this book, Levinas asks us to imagine an event, though one we would not ordinarily encounter in our lives, where everything that we normally relate to, and that gives a certain permanence and stability to our existence, disappears. The question would be, what remains after this disappearance? There would still be an experience, but no longer the experience of something, since everything has dissolved; rather it would be the experience of the very nothingness left behind by the dissipation of the things. There are certain moments in our lives, Levinas argues, when it could be said that we have had such an experience of nothingness. One might conceive of it in this way. Imagine that the world in which one lives, the daily rounds of one's life, was like a picture or a photograph in which everything had its place. Imagine that this picture or photograph, through some kind of bizarre change, started to dissolve, that all the things represented there began to run into one another and disappear until you were finally only left with the blank negative. This absence would be the experience of the 'there is', as though behind the solidity of each thing there lurked, like a fog or mist, the possibility of it vanishing into a void.

Such an experience is not a factual event. It is not as if the things actually disappear, and this experience arises only in certain moods. In such moods, our existence is torn from its everyday involvement with things, so that for the first time it can emerge from behind them. I am no longer related to this or that thing or to this or that possibility, but to existence itself. This is the ontological significance of the 'there is' (for the meaning of 'ontology', see the ontology box on p. 54). It is the disclosure of our existence unencumbered by our attachment to things. In the 'there is' we come face to face with our being, which is literally 'no-thing' at all.

Insomnia, Levinas tells us in *From Existence to Existents*, is an example of such an existential mood (for the meaning of 'existential', see the existentialism box on p. 48). It can happen that in the middle of the night, when the effort of falling asleep no longer seems feasible, and when your whole body aches and your consciousness is exhausted, that your room takes on a terrible and dreadful aspect. It seems that the things themselves in the room, the table you sit at during the day, and the wardrobe in which you place your clothes, are decomposing into the night so that it appears as though it is this night that is looking back at you, and no longer your treasured possessions. Still worse, however, still more terrible, is that you yourself seem to be dissolving into this all-enveloping night. Just as there is no place for your belongings and the security and shelter they once seemed to offer, so too there is no place for yourself; everything has disappeared into this frightful night.

Like Levinas, Blanchot also describes the experience of the 'there is' as the experience of the very void or absence in which the things of my everyday world dissolve and disappear. The evaporation of my world in the night of the 'there is' bears witness to the nothingness at the heart of my existence, which the oscillation of activity and rest, the rhythm of the ordinary day and night, does everything to conceal. It is in Blanchot's novel *Thomas the Obscure* that we can find one of the most vivid descriptions of the experience of this 'other night' that is not merely the opposite of the day, but its undoing:

> I discover my being in the vertiginous abyss where it is not, an absence, an absence where it sets itself like a god, I am not and I endure. An inexorable future stretches forth infinitely for this suppressed being. ... Here is the night. The darkness hides nothing. My first perception is that this night is not a provisional absence of light. For from being a possible locus of images, it is composed of all that which is not seen and is not heard, and, listening to it, even a man would know that, if he were not a man, he would hear nothing. In

> true night, then, the unheard, the invisible are lacking, all those things that make the night habitable. It does not allow anything other than itself to be attributed to it; it is impenetrable.
>
> (TO 104)

We can see a connection here concerning this separation between this other night and our daily rhythm, on the one hand, and our earlier treatment of the language of literature, on the other. The day (and the night that belongs to it) is part of the lucidity and clarity of communication, whose ideal is the disappearance of language altogether in the ideas or concepts that it expresses, and the 'other' night is the double absence of literature, which is the negation both of the things themselves and the concepts that represent them. This similarity between the experience of the night and the double absence of literature is made evident when Blanchot writes 'Night is the book: the silence and inaction of the book' (SL 113–14). It is this link that will serve as the clue for finding the meaning of the relation between literature and ethics for Blanchot. Before we can address this directly, however, we need to make sense of the ethical relation to the other, which Blanchot takes and develops from Levinas, and come to see how this relation changes his conception of language.

FROM THE VIOLENCE OF LANGUAGE TO THE ETHICS OF SPEECH

In his earliest critical works, which were primarily the subject of our interpretation of Blanchot in the previous chapters, the relation to language and the world is essentially one of violence: 'In authentic language, speech has a function that is not only representative but also destructive. It causes to vanish, it renders the object absent, it annihilates it' (WF 30). The language of literature extenuates this violence, rather than mitigating it. Not only is the reality of the thing extinguished, but also the referentiality of the concept. In both cases, language is understood as negation. The only difference between the negativity of the concept, where the thing is abolished in the idea, and the negativity of the word, where the idea is abolished in the word, is that the former is a useful negativity, forming the logic by which our world is constructed, whereas the latter is useless or unworkable, decomposing the world in literature's dissimulation.

In *The Infinite Conversation* it is not the interrelation between the thing, concept and word, which is of primary concern, but the ethical relation to the other, and this ethical relation is understood above all as a relation to language; the revelation of the other, Blanchot writes, 'that does not come about in the lighted space of forms belongs wholly to the domain of speech' (IC 55). The important change from the earlier description of language is that now Blanchot is describing the relation implied in spoken and not written language. This difference can be understood as the difference between dialogue and comprehension. The very etymology of the word 'comprehension' (from the Latin *com* + *prehendere* where the latter means 'to grasp') already suggests violence towards things in which the distance between them and me is annulled by the power of understanding. To know is to absorb. In dialogue with the other, on the contrary, it is the distance between the other and me that sustains the conversation. In addressing the other, I do not annihilate their distance so as to reduce them to me; rather, to speak to someone is to respond to their distance. The 'distance' here is not the physical space that separates us, but the ethical difference between us that prevents us from being reduced to the same thing. In the ethical relation I respond to your irreducible presence. This 'response' does not occur through vision but speech. In conversation with you, I approach you in your difference from everyone else. In vision, the distance between the object and the spectator is removed by visibility, whereas in speech, the self and the other remain separate, though still in a relation. Seeing is a relation of unity or fusion, whereas speaking is one of separation or difference. Blanchot describes a conversation with Georges Bataille in the following words:

> What is present in this presence of speech, as soon as it affirms itself, is precisely what never lets itself be seen or attained: something is there that is beyond reach (of the one who says it as much as the one who hears it). It is between us, it holds itself between, and conversation is approach on the basis of this between-two: an irreducible distance that must be preserved if one wishes to maintain a relation with the unknown that is speech's unique gift.
>
> (IC 212)

The unity of seeing is explained by the fact that in comprehension there are not two terms but three: the two terms in relation and the third term that mediates and forms the unity between them. If we go back to our discussion of definitions, then a definition acts as a third term that unifies and annuls the difference between items in a relation. Thus, both you and I, as we remarked in Chapter 1, can be defined as 'rational animals'. Under this definition both you and I become identical. The relation of conversation, on the contrary, is the absence of a third term that would make us the same. We are directly face-to-face to one another. This absence of a third term is the approach of the other in its strangeness or difference from me. It is this difference that Blanchot calls the 'relation to the unknown' that is maintained in speech, but which is lost in comprehension. Of course, it is possible to relate to others not through speech, but as an object of knowledge. I can define, label or categorize them. The other then becomes an object as though it were like any other thing, and rather than language being a response, it is an act of violence. I can say that the other, for example, is a 'Black' or a 'Jew' and refuse to relate to them in their irreducible difference. The violence of language can then lead to violence against others. The other can also be disposed and got rid of like any other object, as for example, Jews were in the Holocaust.

The other approaches me in speech as the stranger and as the unknown, who comes to me from outside and who, in addressing me, undermines my self-repose and certainty. The other does so not from a position of mastery, as though it simply forced me to give up my domination of things through an order or a command, since this would be a continuation of the language of violence in the struggle for ascendancy. On the contrary, the other's address to me constitutes an interruption of the language of violence by the language of peace. The other approaches me, Levinas argues, in dialogue or conversation as destitute and poor, and it is in this very feebleness that it suspends my power and violence. This poverty of the other, which disturbs me right to my inner being as though invaded from the outside, Levinas calls the 'face'. It is this that Blanchot sees as the most crucial aspect of his philosophy. For only the human face can break with the anonymity of existence that risks overwhelming us in its senselessness and absurdity, but does so only because it exceeds every attempt to comprehend and classify it. It does so not because it is absolutely powerful, as though I cringe in fear in the face of the human, but from a position of weakness – it is the suffering of others that demands my response, and it is this response that we first of all name ethics, before any decision or choice:

> The [face] – here is the essential, it seems to me – is that experience I have when, facing the face that offers itself to me without resistance, I see arise 'out of the depths of these defenseless eyes' out of this weakness, this powerlessness, what puts itself radically in my power and at the same time refuses it absolutely, turning my highest power into im-possibility.
>
> (IC 54)

The other interrupts my subjectivity, it does not sustain it, and this is why, for Blanchot, we should not confuse Levinas's ethics with a complacent defence of our moral intentions and the institutions that they underwrite. For ethics is not a matter of the preservation of culture, as we shall see in the subsequent chapters' discussion of politics, but the impetus to its continued critique:

> Responsible: this word generally qualifies – in a prosaic bourgeois manner – a mature lucid, conscientious man, who acts with circumspection, who takes into account all elements of a given situation, calculates and decides. The word 'responsible' qualifies the man of action. ... *My* responsibility for the Other presupposes an overturning such that it can only be marked by a change in the status of 'me,' a change in time and perhaps in language.
>
> (WD 25)

The proximity between literature and ethics is that they both displace the subject through language. Responsibility does not begin in a decision or obligation that is freely chosen by or coerced from a subject. Responsibility means that the other takes my place, such that responsibility, as Blanchot writes, 'is not mine and causes me not to be I' (WD 18). In the same way, in the demand of writing, the 'I' of the author is replaced by the anonymity of language that refers neither to his or her consciousness, nor to the consciousness of the reader, but to an incessant and interminable language that precedes them both. 'The writer', Blanchot writes, 'belongs to a language which no one speaks, which is addressed to no one, which has no center, and which reveals nothing' (SL 26).

So far we have proceeded in this discussion as though Blanchot and Levinas were entirely in agreement about writing and ethics. This is not the case, however. Their divergence lies in how they interpret the relation between writing and speech. There are two topics that we shall discuss in the next sections: first of all, how Blanchot's understanding of writing differs from Levinas's, and, second, how out of this different understanding of writing he develops what he calls the experience of the 'neuter'.

THE DIFFERENCE BETWEEN SPEECH AND WRITING

For Levinas, there is only the language of ethics, which is interlocution or interpellation, and the language of comprehension and reason. The second corresponds to what, in our explanation of Blanchot's theory of language, we called information. It is because Levinas can only think of writing as a tool for the preservation or storage of information that he also interprets it as unethical. We need to be able to see why this is not necessarily the case, if we are to think about the difference between writing and speech at a more profound level.

When we think about speech ordinarily we imagine two speakers and what is said between them. Similarly, when we think about writing, we picture the writers and the marks that they leave on the page and perhaps subsequently the reader who interprets them. This is not how Blanchot portrays the difference between speech and writing in *The Infinite Conversation*. He does not deny these ordinary conceptions, rather he wants to probe these relations (the two speakers in conversation, the writer and the page, the reader and the page) so that a strange complicity between speech and writing emerges. It is in this involvement between speech and writing that Blanchot begins to diverge from Levinas. For the latter sees writing as profoundly unethical and thus utterly opposed to the relation of speech. Thus for Levinas, at least in his earlier work, there can be no relation between the demand of literature and ethics as Blanchot conceives it.

Levinas cannot see this connection because his work continues within a certain traditional conception of writing. Let us say a little more about this conception so that we might be better able to make out these different relations of speech and writing. We can interpret Levinas's work as making a distinction between two conceptions of speech, and Blanchot follows him in this regard. In one conception of speech, conversation is merely the transmission of information between two speakers. In a certain sense, what matters in this relation is not who speaks, but what is said. Levinas wants to invert this traditional order of priority, by giving precedence to the speakers in the relation, rather than what is said. It is the presence of speakers to one another in language that is the condition for ethics. Nonetheless this ethical conception of language, with which Blanchot concurs, and which is to be distinguished from the informational conception of language, carries the very same notion of writing as the latter does, because it sees in writing not the presence of interlocutors to one another, but only the carriage of information.

Without disagreeing with Levinas, Blanchot changes the description of the relation of speech, bringing it into closer proximity with the relation of writing as he conceives it. On the one hand, he changes the relation of speech away from its emphasis on the other person to the relation of 'otherness', and, on the other, he changes the conception of writing from its emphasis as information to its experience as literature. Although the first part of *The Infinite Conversation*, 'Plural Speech' (interestingly subtitled 'the speech of writing') contains a masterful interpretation of Levinas's ethics, his own description of the relation of speech is subtly different. Here our attention is not drawn to the other as the other person, but to the relation of otherness itself, which draws both speakers into a strange space that dispossesses them of their self-identity and repose. This is why the description of the opening conversation of *The Infinite Conversation* focuses on the weariness through which both speakers speak to one another, and how this weariness places them outside the ordinary relations between people (IC xiii–xxiii), rather than on the speakers themselves.

It would be wrong to suggest that this subtle change of emphasis marks a disagreement between Blanchot and Levinas; rather, it allows the former to bring the relation of speech closer to the relation of writing. For what is decisive is not so much the presence of the other as another person, but the strangeness of the relation itself in which the other person is present, and which places that other person outside the ordinary relations of language. If one sees writing merely as information, as certainly Levinas does in his early work, then it is difficult to conceive how it could be brought into proximity with this strangeness. But if you do not; that is to say, if you think of writing as literature, as Blanchot does, then this proximity does not seem inconceivable. To see why, we need to go back to our first discussion of language.

In Blanchot's view, as we remember, language is to be understood as negation. The word is the negation of the physical thing, for the sake of an idea that expresses it. It then becomes something that can be communicated. It can pass, so to speak, from one mouth to another. The physical reality of the thing is transformed into something ideal, and it is as this ideality that it belongs to the unity and totality of thought. But as we have already seen in Chapter 2, the absence of the written word is not only the external form of the idea, but also its corruption. This is because writing is both the absence of the thing and the idea. Writing is no longer simply a tool for the externalization and preservation of thought, but is the exposure of thought to language that transgresses its own unity and totality. Language as writing is the experience of dissipation, loss and dispersal, where language is not something at the disposal of thought from within, but confronts it with an 'outside'. Therefore, it places the writer and the reader in a relation of strangeness to the text that is analogous to the relation of speech. In both cases, language is no longer the expression of a potent subjectivity, but its reversal in the exposure to the exteriority of language. For Blanchot, both his understanding of literature and Levinas's of ethics belong to this exteriority, and literature is one way in which it can be approached. This drawing near to the outside of language will be the topic of the next section.

THE NARRATIVE VOICE

The possibility of approaching this 'outside' is given to us by literature. There is no general experience of language as language, since what is general belongs to language's subordination to thought; only the work of literature is the experience of language as language, but since it is thought that reduces language to universal meanings, literature only experiences language in the singular. For this reason, literature does not give us a definition of language, but every work struggles to re-invent language once again. This singular experience is the experience of the anonymity of language that seems to be spoken by no one, and which Blanchot calls the neuter. This neutrality of language is not to be confused with objectivity of thought, for it is not a neutrality that the subject has the power to evoke within itself as the anonymous voice of authority, where it becomes the mouthpiece for a universal truth; rather it is the expression of language itself outside signification, prior to the discourse of either the written or spoken word.

In *The Infinite Conversation*, Blanchot describes the neuter of language that emerges in literature as the narrative voice. We might think that it is the voice of the writer, and undoubtedly there are some books where the presence of the author's voice seems very real indeed. And yet in such instances, are we sure whether we are reading literature at all, and not just obsessions of the author that have been disguised through the beliefs and opinions of the characters? The literature that appears to be touched most intimately by the exteriority of language expresses a language that escapes both the writer and the reader. It is language pushed to the limit of communication, or which communicates so apparently limpidly and effortlessly, like the short stories of the contemporary American writer Raymond Carver (1938–90), that in this communication something 'unsayable' seems to emerge, a mysterious thickness or density of the word. This disappearance of authors in the words that they write must be distinguished from the way that the individual vanishes in the objectivity of thought. In this latter case, the thinker dissolves into the concepts that he expresses, whereas in the former, it is the words themselves that appear to come to the fore. In the first case, the thinker disappears into the unified field of thought in general, whereas in the second, the author disappears so that it is not the unity and objectivity of thought, but language itself that is expressed. This is why we say that every work of literature, to the extent that it exposes itself to the demand of writing, expresses language in its own singular way.

The narrative voice, then, is not the externalization of the inner thoughts of the writer, but the unfolding of language. The author experiences this, Blanchot writes, as the movement of the 'I to the he' (IC 380–1). What does the 'he' here refer to? It does not refer to another person, like the personal pronouns 'I' and 'you', as though someone were writing in my place or reading in yours, but the very indistinctness of the narrative voice that seems to refer to no one (it might be important to note here that in French 'il' can mean both 'it' as well as 'he'). It is as though the voice were coming from so far away that it could be barely heard and could no longer be attached to a person at all. The anonymity of the narrative voice is not to be confused with the distance of the author from the text who, because of certain aesthetic aims, chooses not to intervene in the telling of the story, but rather this anonymity constitutes the very isolation of the text from both the reader and the writer. It is as though this voice, which is only faintly discerned, were coming from the text and from outside of this world. The 'he' of the narrative voice is not the substitute for any person or individual, nor even an imagined 'he' that is supposed to be telling the story, rather it is the marker for the very anonymity of literature:

> Narration that is governed by the neutral is kept in the custody of the third-person 'he', a 'he' that is neither a third person nor the simple cloak of impersonality. The narrative 'he' (*il*) in which the neutral speaks is not content to take the place usually occupied by the subject, whether this latter is a stated or an implied 'I' or the event that occurs in its impersonal signification. The narrative 'he' or 'it' unseats every subject just as it disappropriates all transitive action and all objective possibility.

> (IC 384)

The difference between the anonymity of the narrative voice and the anonymity of knowledge is that the latter is merely a function of the structure of the subject that enables us to distinguish between the content of the thought and the thought itself. This is given to us in the difference between the word and the concept. The anonymity of the narrative voice, on the contrary, comes from outside the subject and for this very reason can only be experienced as something singular and unrepeatable, when the words are separated from the concept. The subject is no longer the master of language, as though it were merely a tool through which I express my thoughts, rather the subject is exposed to language as though language had its own *exteriority* that had nothing to do with my discourse. I experience this exteriority as the resistance of literature to comprehension. What recoils against me is language as the neuter, which is neither spoken nor written by anyone. It is the murmur or rustling of language, as it is described by Samuel Beckett in *The Unnameable* and which Blanchot quotes in his essay on the same author 'Where Now? Who Now?' (1953):

> The words are everywhere, inside me, outside of me ... I hear them, no need to hear them, no need of a head, impossible to stop them, impossible to stop. I'm in words, made of words, others' words, what others ... the whole world is here with me, I'm in the air, the walls, the walled-in one, everything yields, opens, ebbs, flows, like flakes. I'm all these flakes, meeting, mingling, falling asunder, wherever I go I find me, leave me, go towards me, come from me, nothing ever but me, a particle of me, retrieved, lost, gone astray, I'm all these words, all these strangers, this dust of words, with no ground for their settling, no sky for

their dispersing, coming together to say, fleeing one another to say, that I am
they, all of them, those that merge, those that part, those that never meet ...

(SS 198)

With this image of a language as murmuring and rustling, we might
finally see why, for Blanchot, writing and ethics are not opposed to one
another. Literature is not ethical because it might have a moral or political message to impart, for even if there is a moral or political element
in the work, then this element is itself subjected to the demand of
literature, which is the negation of the world of action. If the writer
attempts to subvert this demand, then the work compromises itself in
becoming didactic, wishing to teach us a moral or political lesson. On
the contrary, it is precisely because literature does not have a message
that it is ethical and political for Blanchot. The link between the ethical
and writing is that both effect a displacement of the subject. In ethics,
the subject is called into question by others, whose exorbitant presence exceeds any comprehension I might have of them, and in writing
the 'I' is exposed to the exteriority of language beyond the unity and
coherence of its own thought. In this way, by linking writing and
ethics, Blanchot both remains with and goes beyond his friend Levinas.
In the chapters that follow we shall see that this relation between
writing and ethics will be deepened through the question of politics.

SUMMARY

Commencing with the articles published in *The Infinite Conversation*
(1969), there is an increasing change in direction and style in Blanchot's
work. First of all, the distinction between his critical and fictional work
becomes increasingly blurred, and, second, ethics and politics come more
than ever to intrude upon his approach to the question of the meaning of
literature. With respect to ethics, the pivotal figure is *Emmanuel Levinas*.
The first connection between their work is the phenomenon of the *'there
is'* which describes the mood in which my world can disappear in the
nothingness of existence. But the most important link is Levinas's
description of the ethical relation to the other. This describes a different
understanding of language than Blanchot's earlier grasp of language as
violence, where the word is both the negation of the thing and the concept,
and in which the stability of my world vanishes in the dissimulation of

language (this also shows the connection of Blanchot's first conception of language with the phenomenon of the *'there is'*). In the relation to the other, *speech* is not understood as violence, but as the presence of the *other* who calls into question my self-repose. This 'response' to the *other* is the true foundation of responsibility, rather than the defence of moral values. It is in this refutation of the *subject* that Blanchot sees the link between writing and ethics. In this sense he differs from Levinas, who sees *speech* and *writing* as being opposed to one another, since he wrongly interprets writing as *information*. For Blanchot, writing is the exposure of both the writer and the reader to the *outside* of language. This *outside* of language is the *voice* that comes from the other side of the subject and is spoken by no one. Elsewhere Blanchot calls this *outside* of language the *neuter*. Both the *other* and *neuter* are words for Blanchot that describe a language that is no longer governed by the primacy of the subject. This is the essential and most important link between ethics and literature, rather than any moral lesson a literary text might have.

6

BLANCHOT AS NATIONALIST

The pre-war writings

In this chapter we will investigate what has become known as the scandal of Blanchot's pre-war writings. He worked throughout the 1930s as a journalist for various right-wing papers. While there are few signs of racism or fascism in these writings, he has been indicted mainly by association with papers that included many anti-Semitic articles. There are two responses to Blanchot's journalistic writings. Either these are ignored completely or they are used to condemn all of his writings. But both these responses are not quite satisfactory. Instead the question really is in what sense Blanchot's politics has its origin in the 1930s and what implications this has on the reception of the more well-known Blanchot who engaged in politics during the late 1950s and 1960s on the side of the left, particularly in the revolt of 1968.

MAY 1968

The revolt of 1968, starting and being mainly confined to France, originally began with Parisian students demonstrating against the closure of a left-wing university in Paris, coinciding with demonstrations against the Vietnam War. Its motivations lay in the repression by the conservative government of General Charles de Gaulle, the insight that the liberation of

France after the Second World War had not led to the hoped-for liberation of French society and the realization that the expected progression of the emancipation of the working class had not taken place. It was hence a revolt against unemployment, poverty and social injustice. The street battles started on 3 May around the famous inner-city university, the Sorbonne, with clashes between students and police units. From here the unrest spread quickly throughout Paris and then to the rest of the industrial centres of France. By now the revolt had reached other countries of Europe. German students began to revolt as well and the street battles spread to Frankfurt and Berlin. A few weeks later about 12 million French workers were on strike and what had begun as street battles between 300 students and the police had become a movement that had a lasting effect on the political landscape of western Europe.

BLANCHOT'S JOURNALISM OF THE 1930s

During the last decade, what has produced the greatest interest in Blanchot's work has not been his subtle and profound approach to the interrelation of literature, death and ethics, but his journalistic writings of the pre-war years, characterizing his first political involvement. We have already mentioned this 'scandal' in the introduction to this book, and an understanding of Blanchot's political thinking requires a reflection on this phase. Blanchot started his publishing career by writing literary and political criticism for extreme right-wing papers. What is seen as scandalous is not so much what Blanchot wrote himself, but that some of the articles in these papers were anti-Semitic. The outrage caused by these facts might have quickly disappeared if it were not also linked to other scandals that rocked the literary establishment; specifically the discovery that the eminent American critic Paul de Man (1919–83) had also in his youth, when he lived in Belgium during the German occupation, written for extreme right-wing anti-Semitic journals. Furthermore, many literary critics in the school of deconstruction were highly influenced by Martin Heidegger, who had supported the German Nazi Party from 1933 to 1934. For some people, the whole critical movement of literary deconstruction can be tarred with the same brush, since Jacques Derrida (and we can safely ignore the fact that he is Jewish) is clearly indebted to Blanchot, and was a close friend of Paul de Man. Such reasoning is obviously absurd and often used to discredit a thought instead of making the attempt to understand it on its own terms. On the other hand, it makes good stories for newspapers. This does not, however, allow us simply to turn our backs upon Blanchot's pre-war journalism and its implications for his conception of the relation between politics and literature.

These early writings have been fairly well documented and are freely available. Nonetheless it is quite clear that a conspiracy of silence surrounded them in France, most likely to avoid the uncomfortable questions they would raise. Although in the 1950s and 1960s Blanchot's writing had an enormous and unparalleled influence on the French intelligentsia, it was as if Blanchot's earlier political stance had been completely forgotten. Thus in the 1966 issue of the leading journal *Critique* dedicated to Blanchot's work, and containing such eminent writers as Michel Foucault and Paul de Man, there is no mention at all of Blanchot's past. We might be tempted to justify such silence by Blanchot's own theory of the anonymity of writing. What is written does not belong to the writer, therefore we should not search for its meaning in the life of the author. But even such an interpretative position does not demand that we should be silent about an author's life and ignore the ethical responsibilities of the writer.

It is, therefore, important not to forget Blanchot's past and to follow up this question for the relation between his early writings and his later engagement with the far left. Our disagreement with his critics is not that Blanchot's political writings are of no importance, but their rash insistence that they have to be seen as the central truth of both his literary criticism and his novels or narratives. Such a claim flies in the face of everything that we can learn from reading Blanchot, who argues that no text can be reduced to a single 'truth' that finds its origin in biographical details of an author's life. Moreover, arguing that Blanchot's opinions from the 1930s determine his whole thought actually obscures the complexity of his political stance.

In order to typify Blanchot's early writings, we need to understand the social situation of France in the 1930s. In France, as in the rest of Europe, there were huge social tensions arising from mass unemployment, the polarization of society and the threat of war. In this environment, liberal democracy seemed to have failed and politics divided into the two extremes of right and left. French nationalism had its own tradition, quite distinct from both Italian and German fascism. While it did contain fascist elements, these were by no means as forceful as elsewhere. Thus, it was entirely possible (as in Blanchot's case) to be a French right-wing nationalist and still violently opposed to the German fascists: fascism is not monolithic. It was also perfectly possible to be a right-wing nationalist without being anti-Semitic, even though anti-Semitism, for the most part, characterized nearly all the French fascist movements, the more so as Léon Blum, the liberal president of the French republic from 1936–7, was Jewish.

Blanchot's commitment to right-wing politics was motivated above all by his opposition to the politics of compromise that characterized the liberal democracy of the day, and which he believed was incapable of defending France against its rising and strengthening neighbours, especially Germany and Russia. As a response, Blanchot repeatedly called for a revolution aimed at a violent overthrow of the liberal state. The greatest threat, for him, were the moderates who governed France, for they acted as if entirely oblivious to the dangers that threatened the nation, lulling everyone into a false sense of security. This is especially so, for Blanchot, in their almost complete ignorance of the threat of Hitler and France's total unpreparedness for what Blanchot saw, and was proved right, as the imminence of war. But why would such an insight commit him to the right side of the political spectrum? Here in the 1930s, in complete contrast to his later political writings, Blanchot subscribed to the nationalistic idea that the community of a nation can only be founded on a myth determining the grandeur of its destiny. In this respect only did his politics have a similarity with the developments that took place in Germany and Italy at the same time. It is in the light of such a return to a founding myth, that he tries to legitimate a language that calls for violence and blood, deemed necessary to escape the decadence of his contemporary France. As we will see in the last chapter, it is precisely such a position that he will decry most vehemently in his later writings. Indeed, when, in a text called 'Intellectuals under Scrutiny' (1984), he apologizes for these writings, this apology is motivated by the insight that, while his nationalistic writings had supported a politics built on myth in order to oppose the elimination of the political sphere in favour of questions of economics, such a nationalistic politics leads precisely to the very abolition of politics against which he had thought to direct it.

'THE IDYLL'

Beyond the actual political situation in the 1930s we can see here already that Blanchot's critique of liberal democracy is motivated by the latter's tendency towards an unobtrusive functioning of the public sphere and hence its implicit abolition of the political as such. Blanchot's early engagement against the inter-war democracy of France is based on his criticism of capitalist society as driven by an ideology of management, that is, against the disappearance of the political in favour of its reduction to questions of economy. It is this critique that remains at the heart of all his political criticism, early and late. Next to the political institutions, the forces of culture are as well informed by a 'fascination of unity' (F 72). The unity of society and culture, in turn, demands the understanding of the singular human being as an atom of the whole, that is as an individual. But the idea of the individual is, as Blanchot says, nothing but an abstraction on the part of a debilitating liberalism (UC 18).

This seems to be contradictory. Do we not understand the idea of democracy as the idea of the universality of freedom, while nationalism seems to appear as a political form denying freedom to the many? We will see in the following why Blanchot sees in liberalism rather a concealed form of totalitarianism, while the continuity of his critique, from his early right-wing involvement to his later engagement on the side of the radical left, will make clear that his nationalism served only as a platform for the interruption of that totality. In other words, for Blanchot, politics in the twentieth century presents itself as necessarily revolutionary, as breaking into the unobtrusive functioning of society. In this respect, political engagement ought to disrupt society in a similar way as the appearance of a stranger disrupts the homogeneity of the home. In the case of the stranger, society will attempt to assimilate him or her, while in order to remain a foreigner, such assimilation has to be resisted. The stranger has to disrupt society in order to remain herself, while a society that claims to be open to strangers has to be able to cope with them without attempting to reduce what is specific to them as strangers.

We can see this point enacted in Blanchot's first story, 'The Idyll' (1936; in SBR 5–33), written at a time when he was presumably supporting xenophobic views. Here we see Alexandre Akim, a foreigner brought to a hospice, incarcerated in a nameless society's prison. But the strange point is that this prison is a rather idyllic community, the foreigners are all well received, are given the opportunity to wash and to feed themselves, and all that is expected in return is some work, not much, but completely meaningless. The proprietors of the asylum seem friendly and happy, the inhabitants of the next village always open and welcoming. While being warned by others that not all is as it seems, it is quite difficult for Akim to see any danger. Now and then punishments of one or other of the inmates who were not so assiduous in their duties takes place, but always accompanied by an air of regret. The community of supervisors and foreigners in the hospice is very strange indeed. It moves from gentleness to brutality without mediation, but always apologetically, so that it is difficult to separate oppressors and oppressed. As Blanchot will say in a later text, the question of injustice does not occur between individuals. While all feel justified in what they are doing, it is only the system that is conscious (F 66–7). Rather, the problem seems to consist in that, here in 'The Idyll', society demands integration and punishes all deviance. What is absolutely forbidden is to interrupt the homogeneity of this society. The foreigner is accepted, not as foreigner, but as one example of a human being given the chance to become integrated into the totality of a society. The danger of this liberal society is that its fascination with unity drives it to totalitarianism. Alexandre Akim wishes to become a part of a community, which would make his freedom possible, but not of a totality without community, that is, a state whose totality suppresses the ethical relation between its citizens. In order to speak of an ethical relation, one has to account for the actuality of the different people involved, rather than thinking about it merely in terms of the formal relation between different tokens of the type 'human being'. Thus the society in which Akim finds himself seems to be open to foreigners, but only as long as they are willing to conform to the idea that it has of a 'human being'. Yet, this idea of the 'human being' is often but a generalization of the population's self-understanding and therefore demands of the foreigner that she give up her identity in order to become 'one of us'. For example, we might say 'all human beings', while our idea of the human being is just that of an English person in the twenty-first century.

Akim describes his new home to a few newcomers in the following words, and we can read this exclamation as an allegory on our modern liberal democracies:

> You'll learn that in this house it's hard to be a stranger. You'll also learn that it's not easy to stop being one. If you miss your country, every day you'll find more

reasons to miss it. But if you manage to forget it and begin to love your new place, you'll be sent home, and then, uprooted once more, you'll begin a new exile.

(SBR 24)

Thus, when the city offers him naturalization by way of marriage, he declines and attempts to escape. Since this escape puts society into question, when Akim is recaptured, he is punished by death. In a strange way, then, he has achieved his freedom in the eyes of the others by way of his death, which expresses the interruption of the unitary society. As a foreigner, Alexandre Akim stands for the other human being insofar as it is experienced as other (see Chapter 5). As Blanchot says, thereby defining the main problem of politics, 'only man is absolutely foreign to me' (IC 60). In the familiarity of a world of objects, in which I orient myself by deliberate action, the other appears as a disruption. The foreigner is then the image of the other human being. Accordingly, the question of politics appears as the question of a community's ability to welcome the other as other, that is, to exist through its continuous interruption. Or rather, from the point of view of political engagement, the determining question of politics appears in the 'call to go out, into an outside' (BR 202), as Blanchot writes in 1968. It is in this respect that political engagement will always remain, before and after the war, revolutionary. The idea of permanent revolution is that of a constant disruption of the tendency of society towards an indiscriminate totality. It is in this respect that Blanchot often refers to the importance of the revolt of 1968, because, not based on an alternative ideology, it constituted a pure political interruption.

A FIRST WITHDRAWAL FROM POLITICS

The beginning of the Second World War brought an end to Blanchot's open political engagement. First of all, war suppresses the possibility of political engagement in its reduction of such engagement to military means. But, second and more specifically, the Second World War changed the realm of politics for all time. If politics concerns the relation to the other as other, then the existence of the extermination camps – an extermination of a people whose persecution had always been based on their being conceived of as insisting on their otherness – is an absolute event that interrupts the political sphere. This absolute event has put the whole of European culture and rationality as a positive force of civilization into question. It is for Blanchot of an all-determining significance, so much so that it will even be the surface motivation for his second withdrawal from political engagement, namely when the French left, in 1969, begins to identify with the struggle of the Palestinians against the state of Israel. Indeed, one might say that his political convictions will become progressively related to the cause of Judaism.

It is difficult to say when exactly Blanchot's drift from the extreme right to the radical left took place. While the war years certainly played a decisive part, already the difficulty of completely feeling at home on the far right, characterized as it is by xenophobia and anti-Semitism, would have precipitated this move, especially because he was already in the 1930s in confrontation with the more fascistic elements of the right. Maybe the most decisive point in the development of his political thought came through his friendship with the French writer Georges Bataille, which began during the war. It is in response to Bataille's reflection on community that Blanchot henceforth develops his political thought.

Blanchot did not openly engage in political discussion between 1937 and 1958, when the ascension to power by General Charles de Gaulle forced him to take a stance. Some commentators have remarked on what they call the irony that Blanchot returned to politics at a time when his former political ideas were finally put into practice. In protesting against the rise to power of General Charles de Gaulle and his right-wing government, he might seem to be working against his own right-wing convictions of the past. But such a remark fundamentally misconstrues Blanchot's political position on account of a preconceived idea of what it means to be 'on the right' or 'on the side of democracy'. This is not to defend his political stance of the 1930s but only to say that, both before and after the war, Blanchot would have opposed a chauvinistic force such as General de Gaulle's in the same way as he distanced himself from the provisional government of France, called the Vichy regime, during German occupation. The Vichy government, led by right-wingers, attempted to reconcile the French with the idea of collaboration with the Germans, thereby implicitly legitimating the occupation. Neither does Blanchot's withdrawal from politics in 1937 indicate his shame over having been involved with the far right, thus withdrawing into the innocent realm of literature and literary criticism. Indeed, his writings of the intermediate period remain highly political. Reading *Faux pas*, a first selection of essays printed in 1943, but especially *The Work of Fire* (1949), it is quite obvious that his engagement with literature always remains an engage-ment in political terms: 'to write is to engage oneself – to call into question one's existence, the world of values – ' (WF 26). A writer cannot forget about the political. As Blanchot writes in 1959: 'it is

true: when two writers meet, they never talk about literature (fortu-
nately); their first remarks are always about politics' (SBR 453). The
political, for a writer like Blanchot, is always very closely related to the
question of literature, which is not to say that an author has to or even
should in her or his activity as a writer take a position in terms of political events. But we will return later to the question of the engagement
of the writer.

While it is, then, often claimed that Blanchot withdrew into 'the
world of literature', conceived in radical distinction from the political,
we will see in the following that, for Blanchot, there is an essential link
between literature and the question of politics. While it is true that his
position between 1937 and 1958 is characterized by a withdrawal from
any active involvement in political questions, it is still with justice that
he can open *The Unavowable Community* (1983) with the words 'I would
again take up a reflection never in fact interrupted … concerning the
communist exigency' (UC 1).

From 1958 onwards Blanchot's engagement is in a movement of the
radical left. It is here that he reflects on the essential part that literature
plays in the realm of the political, driving at a formulation of 'literary
communism'. In order to understand this development, we will have
to enter into his critique of liberal democracy, of the 'information
society', then bring out the essential role that literature plays in respect
to the community of human life before we will finally be able to reflect
on his problematization of the ideas of politics, community and
communism. In the brevity of this exposition we might not always be
able to trace the temporal development of Blanchot's thought. Our
intention is rather to show its underlying unity.

SUMMARY

The 'scandal' associated with Blanchot's political engagement in the
1930s raises the more important question of the unity of a writer's life and
his or her work. Here we can see that, while Blanchot's political orienta-
tion changes radically between the 1930s and the 1950s and 1960s, what
remains is his criticism of liberal democracy as a force that leads to an
abolition of the political in its reduction to the administration of public
affairs. Yet, Blanchot himself will come to see a 'scandal' in his early
political views, insofar as they demanded a return to a mythical founda-

tion of the community, which he later realizes leads to the same reduction of political life.

7

ETHICS AND POLITICS

In this chapter we will trace the origin of Blanchot's political thought in his reflection on the ethical situation. That is to say, while all political thought involves considerations concerning the way that human beings live in community, often this only extends to predicting how people will react to certain political or economic ideas. Consequently, much of contemporary political thought has reduced itself to questioning how best to organize the economy. Blanchot's criticism mainly bears on such reductive conceptions of politics, and we will show that any political thought not informed by a consideration of the nature of human community, not only as that which it governs, but as its own foundation, will finally proceed to abolish political life itself.

Politics is traditionally conceived of as the rule of law and the history of political institutions, of the distribution of power within and between societies, as the development of military pacts through war and peace. A course on politics would not normally deal with the community of human beings beyond the questions of its organization and the distribution and redistribution of wealth, power, services and food supplies. As long as it concerns itself with the language of the community as such, for example, with propaganda and communication, it will do so only in order to show how power is accumulated and exerted. In other words, when we generally speak about politics, we do not reflect on what makes a community of human beings possible.

Speaking of the life of a community we think solely of production, work and action, and often forget to enquire into the very possibility of human community. Generally speaking we take the existence of such a community for granted and discuss solely the question of how it should be organized.

But what is it that makes a community possible? We entertain many different relations with diverse other human beings every day, and we can easily see that all of these are mediated by language. We talk to a shopkeeper in order to receive certain goods. We are talked at by a lecturer so that we come to understand a certain theory. We talk to our friends in order to discuss the latest political events. In Parliament, politicians argue about the best form of a law. All these relations take place on the anonymous level of the everyday, where 'one' speaks with or to 'others'. Indeed, most of our days are filled with this community of language, even those moments when we sit alone in front of a television set and listen to the lives of imaginary others talking to each other. The human community rests on communication by way of language. Through media and personal experience, our lives seem more and more engulfed by such forms of linguistic communication. As we have seen in Chapter 5 on the language of ethics, such modes of communication are not 'added' to our existence as individuals. Rather we become individuals by being inserted into this community of language. Consequently, such linguistic communication makes up the very nature of our existence.

Mostly, and we have seen this already in Chapter 3 through Heidegger's critique of the everyday situation, in which I suffer the insight that I can be replaced in respect to anything that I am, we deal with other human beings as familiar items within our everyday world. We think of others in the sense that we include them in the planning of our lives. When I want to go to the cinema, I think which friend to ask, so that I do not have to go alone. If I want to book a holiday, I think about how to keep the travel agent happy, so that he might find the best deal for me. If I try to win a game, I attempt to guess the moves and schemes of my competitors in order to counteract them in time. If I buy shares, I consider what people will buy in the future. As far as all these activities are concerned, other human beings are part of my world, where the word 'world' is understood as the totality of the knowledge I have of my situation and its circumstances. Here I mostly treat the other as analogous to things; I objectify her or his behaviour, I calculate their possible actions and plans, and I mostly do this by way of experience and by stipulating that they are human beings just like me. That is to say, my understanding of others is a mixture of identifying them with myself and of correcting this identification on account of past experiences of others behaving in a way that I had not then foreseen. The same holds true for the political arena in which laws are forged and decisions taken.

From here we can see why the question of politics is closely related to the question of language and literature. Any community begins with what Blanchot terms writing, understood as the origin of language and literature. Power theorized in political terms can be understood as a power of speech, of making one's voice heard and of subduing that of others. But the fact that we can speak rests on our insertion into the linguistic community. Such an account of language as the root of all community and individuality, necessarily sets Blanchot on a path of confrontation with the theories of liberal democracy. This is because liberalism generally presupposes the existence of independent and essentially private individuals, who then enter into exchange with each other, and who only use language as a means of communication. According to these theories, all political questions occur within the realm of our understanding, which is to say that it is there that solutions can be found by calculative means. Blanchot, on the other hand, understands community from the perspective of language and, therefore, as not recoverable by the understanding. From here he infers that human community is itself vulnerable. At one and the same time, because it lies beyond the grasp of the understanding, it is possible to suppress it, by insisting on the sovereignty of the isolated individual, and impossible to affirm it, as there is no incontrovertible evidence for its existence (F 106). This is because, as we have seen, the relation to the other, without whom I am nothing, escapes the realm of the objectivity of the understanding. Consequently, communication, as the relation that characterizes the community, cannot be understood as an exchange of information. And, to be sure, looking more closely at the language of the everyday, as I hear it on the radio or on television, it turns out that its main function does not lie in the transfer of information, for we often do not even listen to it, but in the false promise of communication purveyed through the illusion that 'somebody is speaking to us'.

THE HUMAN RELATION IS TERRIFYING

Saying that politics ultimately resides in the possibility of human communication leads us to understand the political by reflection on the relation to the other. We have seen already that Blanchot thinks of the other as the foreigner. It is for this reason that Blanchot writes that 'the human relation is terrifying' (IC 60). It is terrible, because it is immediate, without a world mediating between one and the other. As long as we see the other just as 'the travel agent' or 'the teacher', functions mediated by the world of utility, we are precisely not relating to the other as other. This immediacy of the relation to the other is Blanchot's interpretation of the concept of 'the face' as we have found it in Chapter 5.

> There is between man and man neither god, nor value, nor nature. It is a naked relation, without myth, devoid of religion, free of sentiment, bereft of justification, and giving rise neither to pleasure nor to knowledge: a neutral relation, or the very neutrality of relation.
>
> (IC 59)

At first surprisingly, we realize that it is the relations that we entertain in the world of utility that make us similar and expendable, while in the immediacy of the ethical relation the other appears as other. We can see here that the totalizing community that we find, for example, among bees or termites, cannot serve as a model for a human community. That is, while these communities are the positive and immanent relations of usefulness subordinated to the good of the whole population, human community presupposes a completely different relation than the communion of its members. The danger of our modern societies, of 'a weary civilisation ... a civilisation in which man has lost hold of himself, no longer able to measure up to the questions that are being asked him by the answers of technical development' is precisely that it gives rise to such an immanent totalitarian state without community (F 79).

But it is easy to see that in order for laws to be passed and political institutions to work, we must presuppose a community between people on account of which these processes can take place. That is to say, in order for an actual discussion between humans to take place, they have to share a common ground. This ground includes their language, their shared history and customs and their experience, which will, having grown up under comparable circumstances, be quite similar. Furthermore, Blanchot claims that the existence of law and political institutions is not necessarily a sign of the existence of a real political community. The other human being is here the object of my deliberations and desires, while the other *as other* has not even yet appeared. These 'other human beings' can be reduced to an anonymous administrative machinery as we find it, for example, in Kafka's novels. The starting thesis of *The Unavowable Community* is, then, that we no longer have any community today.

Blanchot argues that we are first and foremost dealing with the other through objectifying him or her and that, in turn, we both become objects for each other. In this case we find the idea of the immanent community; that is, of a community that lives within a world of objects, reducing the individual human being to relations of knowledge. In this world, I think of my abilities and then offer them on the market of services and emotions. Here we understand ourselves, as well as others, as economic units within everyday relations of exchange. This reduction is also expressed in the idea of the modern community of service providers or stakeholders and we can see how such an idea of the community abolishes the political – as the realm of meaningful human communication – for the sake of economics.

That, as Blanchot says, our age does not even understand the sense of community any longer, is based on the fact that the other, in our societies, no longer appears as other at all. In such relations we are no longer posing the question of politics – but, as we argued, have long reduced it to the question of economics. This is obviously the case in the global community that we have got used to calling the global village, intent on saying that there are no foreigners in this world, but only individuals just like me. This is the main argument against our liberal, capitalist societies: that capitalism is an essentially apolitical movement, because in order to make free markets possible, that which matters to these markets must be understood as freely exchangeable units. But that is to say that these units have to be essentially the same or at least reducible to the same. In such a world, politics can think of the relation between people only as that between selfsame units, so much so that the individual is understood in analogy to a pound coin: there are certain things it can do and that it ought to do, others that are forbidden to it, but essentially all these units are the same and can be exchanged for one another. We therefore no longer speak of an ethical community, but merely about a morally controlled marketplace of human objectifications. The problem lies with our fundamental attitude of theorizing the world, of taking it as something that can be mastered by the understanding. This state of affairs expresses itself today in that we are more and more suspicious of judgement, rather referring decisions back to 'hard facts', as if only the understanding could deliver equality.

> But, are we sure that the 'world' can be thematized? Maybe there is a profound rejection of thematization, which we discern, for example, in the refusal to talk about someone who is close to us, to transform him into a theme, into an object of reflection, accepting only to speak to him.
>
> (L 188)

If the question of community rests on the essential relation between human beings, and if this relation precedes the question of knowledge, then we are thrown out of the realm of traditional political theories.

THE LOSS OF COMMUNITY

Blanchot thinks of our age, characterized by an intensification and globalization of communication, by the media of telecommunications and the 'information super-highway', as one that has lost the sense of community to the degree that it no longer even understands what a community among human beings would be like. In other words, we have lost the sense of community so much that we do not even realize that we have lost any sense of it.

But what about the dream of the global village in which all are equal and united in free communication? Blanchot's most pertinent critique of such illusions can be found in an essay called 'The Great Reducers' (1965; in F 58–72). The argument in this later text is still quite reminiscent of his early reflections during the 1930s and 1940s. Every culture is characterized by a reductive power, which attempts to integrate all dissenting discourses. The examples that Blanchot uses are quite telling. He considers the conferment of the Nobel Prize for literature in 1964 on the French philosopher and literary author Jean-Paul Sartre, which the latter turned down, the 'industry of conscience' in the form of the television and the invention of the paperback book. In terms of the first example, he describes Sartre as a difficult and odd writer, who never pleased the critics in the same way as his contemporary Albert Camus (1913–60) did. That the Nobel Prize committee decided to confer the prize for literature on Sartre's *Words* (1964) can then be understood as an attempt to placate a writer and to ignore the disruption of literature by fitting his work into the canon of the tradition, that is, to make it part of the whole of culture. To offer Sartre the Nobel Prize for literature then means to certify that his work is inoffensive. 'But perhaps what makes literature inconspicuous also spells its doom' (BR 145). As far as Sartre wanted to remain a writer, he then had to turn down a prize that would have committed him to a certain ideology of culture, society and freedom. Literature, once it has become an integral part of the canon, stops communicating. It is more and more seen as an object of which one might study the structure and composition, dissecting it like the corpse it has become.

The same happens in the presentation of culture through the medium of television. It is true that we are today much better informed about political, cultural and other events, but, as Blanchot argues, their meaning is lost in that very medium. At the end of an evening of television, having watched the news, a film and some political commentary, the spectator goes to bed with a feeling of contentment, without anything having taken place. He might remember some facts later, but these events no longer communicate any meaning.

> There should be interesting events and even important events, and yet nothing should take place that would disturb us: such is the philosophy of any established power, and, in an underhanded way, of any cultural service.
>
> (F 67)

Furthermore, television leads to the depoliticization of society insofar as it concentrates life around the home. Every regime has always been fearful of the streets. Human beings discussing and arguing on the streets might form, before they are even aware of it, a critical mass that might at any moment turn into political action. 'The man in the street is always on the verge of becoming political' (IC 240–1). Today it seems no longer necessary to forbid larger gatherings on the streets, as the idea of the television, delivering the world into our living rooms, makes it superfluous to follow the political events in the community of streets and cafes. Here again we can see that for Blanchot the human being is not this or that. Whatever it can become, for example, politically active, depends on the circumstances of its community. If such circumstances are not at all given, then it might not become political, or maybe not even self-reflective and critical. As Blanchot argues, one cannot be an intellectual or a writer on one's own. One could not even exist as a human being outside of community. From here follows the urgency of Blanchot's political engagements: there is no end to the destruction of the human being, insofar as it is nothing (IC 135). But that means as well that one cannot just wait for better times in the comfort of one's home.

The last example Blanchot singles out for his critique is the introduction of the paperback. But what is the paperback? Is it really just a cheap book? One that spreads the word to all parts of society? Blanchot's problem is that with the paperback rises a certain ideology of European culture. The paperback serves the stabilization of political power in two ways: on the one hand, it proclaims that culture is now available to the totality of the population and that it is the whole of culture that is published without restriction. This first point thus concerns the liberality of our societies, which proclaim that there need not be any disruption, because freedom is already won. On the other hand, the production of paperbacks necessitates a different approach in publication. Paperbacks are produced in big numbers and are profitable only if turned over in short time spans. Everything is published and quickly published, but that is to say that no book has enough time to leave an impact on culture. The realm of culture, once thought to develop in rhythms of intervention and disruption, thus inscribing itself as a tradition, no longer expresses itself in the mass-produced paperback. Instead the answer to the problem of the transmission of culture is represented in technological terms, giving rise to the same ideology, which rests on the belief that:

> The technical regulates all problems, the problem of culture and its diffusion, like all other problems; there is no need for political upheaval, and even less need for changes in the social structures.
>
> (F 70)

These reductive powers of our societies have strengthened over the last decades, to a degree that, since 1968, any disruption to the functioning of society has been seen as intrinsically negative. 'The great reducers' have worked to a degree that we stand before the prospect of the abolition of the political and the death of literature. The political sphere, as we see, is nothing but such disruption itself, expressed already in the disruption that I experience in the face of the other.

If every established political power strives toward such abolition of the political, it can be seen that the politics of literature must lie in the idea of permanent revolution. This becomes clearer when bearing in mind that its success will always turn into defeat: if the challenge of a literary work is successful, it will itself be reduced to that which is the norm of communication. While Samuel Beckett's (1906–89) language once shone in its desperation and aridity, today it has become a work read to illustrate our literary heritage. While it appeared as a disruption of our language and society, now we have the feeling that it has positively enriched our culture.

THE ATOMIC BOMB

If the power of culture is intrinsically that of reducing the diversity of the life of the community to its totality, how can there ever have been a history of political communities that only now seems to come to an end? In 'The Apocalypse is Disappointing' (1964; in F 101–8), Blanchot shows that there is one argument that binds the question of technology to this decline of politics. Any given community exists on account of the disruption of its own unity. That is, there is a power of unification, which we call the understanding, and a power of disruption, which we call reason. The understanding moves solely within the world of knowledge, concerning itself with particular things, while the idea of reason constantly exceeds the given, by referring to the whole. If, for example, I apply my understanding to the construction of the atomic bomb, all I have to think of are the particular problems given in the task. I can analyse the problem, cut it up into different parts to be solved by different scientists. If, on the other hand, I apply my reason to any question of justice, I have to bear in mind the whole of existence and my relation to the world and to others. Instead of being able to find a correct answer that can be proven in its application, I have to pass a judgement that can be questioned by everybody and that can find progress only in our communal discussions concerning the idea of justice. One might as well say that understanding calculates the world, while reason is the power of judgement. However, the problem of our modernity is that understanding has been served by the development of technology with powers that reason can no longer master. Reason, which is the higher intellectual power because it is related to the whole, has been left behind by the forces that we have unleashed. Rather than reasserting its superiority over understanding, 'the caption that would best illustrate the blackboard of our time might be this one: The anticipation of reason humbling itself before the understanding' (F 108). But an understanding that does not serve the wider aims of reason is not only positivistic but also nihilistic. Here understanding runs amok; it can always press its cause further, while reason stands by. Not held in check, it tries to understand everything, even the human being itself, and to be able to do so, it has to reduce everything to atoms. The way that it understands the political community is essentially apolitical.

POSITIVISM AND NIHILISM

Positivism encompasses all those philosophies that restrict the interpretation of reality to those things that 'are actually existing'. Thus one of the fathers of positivism, David Hume (1711–76), argued that only those ideas had validity that could be traced back to an actual sense-impression. Consequently ideas like that of God or mathematics, or even that of justice become highly problematical. Later positivists have tended to say that any question that cannot be verified by direct experience is intrinsically meaningless so that it would be nonsensical to seek to answer it. Positivism tends towards scientism and we can further clarify its nature by looking at the logical positivists, who worked about a century ago. Here the question is what actually exists as the basis of scientific investigation. We might think the answer is matter, that which is investigated in experimentation, but logical positivists argue that in scientific developments, what really exists are the sentences uttered or written down by a scientist during any experiment. The fabric of science does then not consist of 'the real world', but of protocol sentences, like 'now hot' or 'here red'. It is quite clear that Blanchot would not receive much praise from positivists. The 'other', the 'neuter', are, according to positivists, completely meaningless words, and even what he calls literature or the political would, according to them, not exist. *Nihilism* is, contrary to first impression, not just the opposite of positivism. Rather, it generally denotes the conviction that nothing is of any value, or even that nothing really exists. Hence the Russian nihilists of the nineteenth century were often accused of declaring that not even human life was of any value. Consequently nihilism is often equated with scepticism. In a more profound way, the German philosopher Friedrich Nietzsche (1844–1900) explained nihilism as a historical phenomenon that arises with the end of the Christian faith. The general belief that 'God is dead' then leads to the end of the belief that a meaningful life is possible. According to both Blanchot and Nietzsche, the latter of which had a profound influence on the former, positivism is one form of modern nihilism. This is because the positivist does not believe in any values, as values 'do not really exist' in form of facts or sense experiences.

The invention of the atomic bomb stands for the second cornerstone of our changing age, where the development of technology has caused this imbalance between reason and understanding. The atomic bomb is, as Blanchot argues, nothing but an image of the overwhelming force of understanding. In other words, it is not the bomb that is the danger, but understanding itself. This is not only true because we might think that such a bomb would not explode by itself or that we might have forgotten to calculate the risk of an accident. Rather, the understanding that produces such a bomb expresses in its production its own image: and it will want to use such a bomb, if only as a threat of being able to use it properly. A bomb is something that takes things apart. An atomic bomb is so good at taking things apart, that it does not even stop at that what we thought were the smallest units of matter; that is to say, atoms. The atomic bomb is thus an image of our growing understanding of natural processes, which also stops at nothing: the understanding functions exactly like a bomb, namely by taking apart what belongs together. When we say that we analyse a problem, we mean that we use our understanding to take it apart into little manageable parts. We thus presume that we can understand whatever problem by taking it apart and considering its single parts in isolation. Such understanding accepts only that of which it can be sure, but it can be sure only of what can be destroyed (F 104). A more contemporary example can be seen in the Human Genome Project. Here the understanding, with the help of a huge scientific apparatus of different scientists and research institutions, takes the human being itself apart, without our being able to say that we know what we are doing. While understanding celebrates its success, reason lies dormant. This is fine for questions of science, or, for example, in order to find out which part of a car is responsible for it not starting; yet such a procedure is dangerous as regards questions of politics, ethics or morality, since the community of human beings cannot be understood as the mere sum-total of all individuals concerned. To solve political problems by way of analysis is, then, to destroy the realm of politics without even realizing that one has done so. It is for this reason that the world is no longer the same since this invention that demands us to think differently, to confront understanding and its positivism wherever it oversteps the narrow margin of its genuine ability.

At the end then, the only hope lies in that 'there still are points of resistance: politics, the play of desire, poetry, thought. These points have grown weak but have not given way' (F 62). If literature is to revive its essentially ethical and political nature, it has to remember that it is essentially a power of contestation.

> Contestation of the established power, contestation of what is (and of the fact of being), contestation of language and of the forms of literary language, finally contestation of itself as power.
>
> (F 67)

In such contestation art turns against the world of established values and it is in this sense that such art can be called the real realm of politics in opposition to the administration of the public sphere, which we are used to call by that name. Art is then the inverted world and, precisely for that reason, cannot be seen as an activity manipulating the real:

> Here in the world subordination reigns: subordination to ends, to measured proportion, to seriousness and order. On one front science, technology, the state; on another, significance, stable values, the ideal of the Good and the True. Art is 'the world turned upside down': insubordination, disproportion, frivolity, ignorance, evil, non-sense.
>
> (SL 216)

SUMMARY

While most contemporary political thought tends to concentrate on questions of economics and the administration of public life, Blanchot argues that all political theory should be based on a reflection on the ethical basis of community. Such reflection brings to our attention the essential unity of the notions of community and communication, making us aware of the centrality of language to any idea of political life. In communication we can see that before we can communicate any explicit meaning we already have to share the implicit world of a language and its written and oral traditions. A community discovers in such political thought that it is as fragile as any actual communication and that it cannot rid itself of this fragility by way of a rigid political system.

The relation to the other human being is analogous to the relation to language. Just as the essential relation to language is a relation prior to the mere exchange of information, the relation to the other human being is only a relation to the extent that I relate to him or her immediately prior to all actual social relations. This immediacy characterizes the relation to the other as other. In this respect, the relation between human beings cannot be thought as the manipulation of quantities and facts. Politics does not arise with the question of how to organize the facts and figures of human coexistence, but takes its point of origin from the community of language and writing. For this reason politics is as much opposed to economic considerations as it is to the powers of culture and institutionalization. But while this holds for the idea of politics generally, the twentieth century has experienced the breakdown of traditional politics, expressed in the existence of the concentration camps and the invention of the nuclear bomb. These have led to the helplessness of political reason and to the reduction of political questions to hard fact, while the fragility of human relations is lost from sight. To clarify this antagonism between politics and the forces of culture, Blanchot uses the opposition between reason and understanding as two faculties of the human mind. While understanding deals with facts in their isolation, reason is the power of judgement, always related to the whole of existence. As the reality of human relations cannot be captured by means of facts, only political reason can counteract the forces of culture that serve as the great reducers of the diversity of human existence. The twentieth century suffers from an overbearing weight placed on understanding and on

relations of fact, as expressed in the rise to power of economics and technology. This means that all our hope, as Blanchot argues, rests with
'politics, the play of desire, poetry, thought' as the points of resistance
against the impoverishment of human relations. Here literature and politics appear as natural allies, pitting their permanent revolution against
the homogenizing forces of culture and the ensuing loss of community.

8

THE LITERARY
COMMUNITY

In this last chapter we shall explore Blanchot's claim that politics can only be thought of in relation to the experience of literature. While the relation between reader and writer serves as a paradigm for the relations amongst human beings, it will emerge that Blanchot's later engagement on the side of the radical left is in step with his reflections on literature and his move towards seeing in Judaism the instantiation of an ethical politics. These points will lead him to a formulation of a 'literary communism', where communism is understood in a more fundamental sense as a politics of continuous interruption.

LA REVUE INTERNATIONALE

It should not come as a surprise to us, since we learned in the last chapter that the relation to the other is a relation exceeding the realm of the known, and as we have seen in Chapter 2 that literature is a discourse of the outside, that Blanchot sees literature and the literary community as a central question in respect to the problem of politics. 'Only man is absolutely foreign to me' (IC 60), as we have quoted above, and, since 'absolutely foreign' means nothing else than lying outside the realm of objective knowledge, we will have to find a medium other than knowledge in order to breach this absolute estrangement. Such a medium we find in art. This weakness, that the human being cannot master the relation to the other, precisely because art does not allow for mastery, is also a strength, or at least a condition of survival. Generally we tend to say that we only have time for art once the base necessities of human life have been looked after. But, originally, art is not a sign of the bourgeois excess of wealth. Blanchot goes as far as proposing that the difference between our successful ancestors and the Neanderthals, who have become extinct, was that the latter seemed not concerned about art, that is, that they never exceeded the animal kingdom (F 9). If we understand the human being as essentially political, we have to see it as essentially artistic. It is in art that we find the origin of the human being and it is therefore in art that we have to look for the essence of the human community.

The idea of the literary community, that is, of the community between writers and readers, seems to take account of the fact that in our modern society we speak of a community of people who have never met each other, and who enter into this community without being mutually present to each other. Rather, the author when writing the text, writes for nobody in particular. Even if she or he has a certain target audience in mind, this audience does not actually exist anywhere. If somebody finally reads the work, this reader will undo all the intentions of the author, appropriating the work even and especially when he attempts to read her or his intentions. In the reader, the author finds her or his undoing, or, as Blanchot says, her or his anonymity. To read a book is, then, to make the author into an author by inaugurating the disappearance of this very author.

This death of the author is intrinsically related to the political dimension of literature. One way to trace this dependency is by following the development of the foundation of the *Revue Internationale* in which Blanchot was deeply involved between 1960 and 1963. Initially it was planned to involve authors from various countries of Europe, while, in the end, it was only the Germans, the Italians and the French who participated in the further planning stages. Finally, there was only one copy edited, namely by the Italian participants, published in Italian in 1964. The attempt of the *Revue* was to find an international medium of a new and engaged literature, a mixture of political texts and short literary texts, mainly in fragmentary form. Already the frag-mentary form, planned and defended by Blanchot, aims at the disruption of the idea of an 'engaged author' professing his political convictions. In the discussion concerning the foundation of the *Revue*,

Blanchot thus argues that the decline of the idea of political '*revues*' goes back to the moment when writers realized that their engagement is muted by writing in the style of the 'personal confession'. The more one speaks from the position of one's own opinions, the less these count in the political arena. Consequently it is precisely the 'engaged author' who loses his engagement by becoming a private person through such statements. The fragmentary form, on the other hand, allows the author to withdraw in favour of the written word, which, speaking without being intoned as the opinion of a particular person, expresses the plurality of public existence. The word begins to communicate as soon as it is cut loose from the particular existence of an author. It is from the fragility of the authorial voice that the word is borne. This is why Blanchot claims that 'it is often when he "is mistaken", when he appears to us to be mistaken, that he manages to speak to us, if we listen well to him, most profoundly' (L 270). This is why literary language is 'properly' political, in that it is only in this separation from a particular subject that the experience of literature can take on an absolute meaning: 'for me, the literary act or experience is indivisible, this act or experience accepts or refuses itself as a whole' (L 269). The proposed *Revue* will then be written in a style that breaks with the idea of authority, even if only the authority of a writer, trying to breathe life into his words. Such a writing is forceful in its political statement, and it is for this reason that Blanchot argues that it develops its disruptive force. The authorities can deal with counter-movements attempting to claim authority for themselves, but they do not know what to do with this 'anonymous community of non-authorizing names'. This is why 'the judiciary authority enforces itself, instinctively, to break it' (L 218).

But it is not only that the relation between writer and reader serves as a model of human relationships generally. Rather, the language of literature is essential to the community, as all community rests on language, and as the language in question is not the everyday language of the exchange of information, but rather the language that gives rise to community. Such language articulates the relation between the members of the community, rather than merely designating things. In other words, all community is originally a literary community. This is also the claim of the book *The Inoperative Community* by Jean-Luc Nancy, which serves Blanchot as a starting point, that any singular human being, if that is you or me, is structured exactly like a literary work

(ICN 78). While this seems a strange comparison to make, we can see many reasons for such a claim. First, like a literary work the meaning of my life is never really determined. Second, to say that I only exist on account of communication with others means that this communication precedes myself. But that is to say that this communication does not actually concern the words that I utter in the presence of others, but that this communication, preceding myself, has always already taken place. It comes from my past, and language, enduring through time, is written language. At the core of myself I thus find an anonymous writing, just as it makes up the literary work.

POLITICS AND THE FACE OF THE OTHER

One way of understanding what Blanchot is trying to do with the idea of politics and the thought of a literary community, is to trace the nearness and distance of his writings to those of the more famous Jean-Paul Sartre, to whom we compared Blanchot's anti-theory in the first chapter of this book. Sartre, like Blanchot, was both a writer of literature and a philosopher. He wrote books of literary criticism as well as plays, novels as well as essays. And, while Blanchot earned his living by writing for various journals, Sartre was involved in the foundation of two journals, one of which has survived to this day as a daily newspaper. Both Sartre and Blanchot have in common that from the 1930s to the 1960s they moved further and further to the political left, and in 1960 they came close to a collaboration on account of the *Revue Internationale*. Both of nearly the same age, there are many similarities between these two writers, down to the topics of their writings and deliberations, and yet, in other ways, they are like night and day. In fact, while Sartre dominated French academic and public life for at least a quarter of a century (see 'Existentialism', p. 48), that is, while the activist Sartre ruled over the French day and was seen wherever anything important happened on the French plane of politics or art, Blanchot belongs to the night that he thematizes. While you will find Sartre in nearly every photograph of intellectuals taken during those years, it is not even clear to most of us what Blanchot looks like. While Sartre used his writings to enhance his activity and hence drew strength out of them, the man 'Maurice Blanchot' vanished behind his texts into insignificance. Even though it appears, in comparison to Sartre's very visible political presence, that Blanchot had withdrawn from the public arena of politics, his true political influence is to be found in the presence of his writings.

Both writers attempt to understand the possibility of human community, presupposing that it necessitates the presence of the other in its own right. But that is to say, as Sartre argues in his most famous philosophical work *Being and Nothingness* (1943), that the other has to be present to me without being either understood as an object of my deliberations, nor as the subject of its actions in the world of knowledge. As long as I regard the other as an object, he does not exist in his own right. As soon as I represent her as a subjective agent, I understand her in analogy to myself and both of us as instances of a universal form of subjectivity. Both, then, think that the other comes from without the world understood in this way, and that he or she therefore breaks into my world. In other words, both think of the other as a 'real transcendence', which is to say as addressing me from beyond my own world and thus no longer on the level of knowledge. If I have power over objects because I can know them, while the other is not an object, than I am essentially passive in relation to the other's presence.

Here again Blanchot is in agreement with Sartre, and it seems that even in terms of the face of the other (see Chapter 5) we find a similar theme. Sartre speaks of the look of the other, by which the other breaks into my world and erodes my power. Indeed, Sartre even speaks of this look as of a sudden hole within the horizon of my world, through which the meaning of my world is taken away from me. Both the face, as much as the look, are beyond the description of the other as either subject or object, in as much as they exceed the relation of knowledge. And still, while the look circumscribes an activity that breaks into my world, the face, insofar as Blanchot understands it, is the sign of passivity, not of the power of another, but of the weakness of myself, of a tiredness that often tends towards a loss of consciousness, to an infirmity of the world. It is not the other's power that subjects me to passivity, but rather the neutrality of the relation. The life of such a community thus often compares to a dream in which one has difficulty moving one's limbs, where one feels persecuted while being unable to run away. Such descriptions of community can be found already in Blanchot's early narratives, like 'The Last Word' (1935; in SBR 35–50) and 'The Idyll' (1936; in SBR 5–33).

As we have argued in the last chapter, the question of politics cannot be separated from that of ethics; we cannot think of the ethical as the place of emotions and feelings, while politics would designate an area of rational understanding. Both these characterizations miss the point of the real life of the community. The ethical relation is the foundation of the political community, and hence the political community has to take account of the fact that the relation to the other is never one of reciprocity. 'I am never facing the one who faces me. ... This inequality is irreducible' (IC 62). This is not to say that the relations in society should be unjust, but that we need another idea of justice.

The ethical stance we have found, as the direct relation between me and the other, makes the other into a foreigner, the one who really is other. I can only deny the other by bad faith, by banishing them (IC 64), since the relation to the other lies before all experience. In this respect, racism, sexism or homophobia cannot be understood as

DIALECTIC

From ancient Greek, literally meaning 'through the tongue', which is to say, by way of discourse or discussion. Originally dialectic concerns the method of gaining knowledge through discourse. This method found its most famous example in Socratic dialogue, written down by Socrates' (469–399 BCE) pupil, the philosopher Plato (427–347 BCE). The main idea here is that the questions and contradictions of your interlocutor enable your argument to develop in a way that would have been impossible to achieve by yourself. In a way, then, the idea of the dialectic is to push language beyond expressing your own opinions to make it say something objectively. From here the idea of the dialectic develops in various forms through the theological discourses of the Middle Ages towards its most famous formulation in Hegel's philosophy. Here the dialectic does not restrict itself to dialogue between two or more interlocutors, rather the contradictions feeding the development of the situation can be found between any of the different parts of reality. For example, what somebody thinks about himself might contradict his actual, material conditions. Hegel then describes how such a contradiction leads to its own resolution. Such a dialectic is called a dialectic of the real, since it is not only our understanding of a situation that is changed, but the situation itself. The critique of Hegel's idea of the dialectic pertains to its ideal of a recognition of universal subjectivity as the end point of human history.

arising from ignorance alone. They require a determination and an act on the part of the racist. This is the fundamental flaw of the Hegelian solution of the dialectic, according to which one begins in ignorance, in order then to proceed to the recognition of the self in the other, a discourse, then, that buys recognition at the price of abolishing all actual life in favour of the universal form of the subject. Indeed, such proclaiming of the discourse of society as driving towards universal equality is not only one shape of totalitarianism in the form of a community based on communion, it is also a lie. In actual fact:

> there is almost no sort of equality in our societies. ... all speech is violence – and to pretend to ignore this in claiming to dialogue is to add liberal hypocrisy to the dialectical optimism according to which war is no more than another form of dialogue.
>
> (IC 81)

Blanchot here takes his leave from communion as the basis of a community.

Our political discourse, characterized by its abstraction from language, speaks about equality in a way that ignores both the disparity between me and the other as the origin of our community, and the actual inequality of our societies. This is why, earlier, we talked about freedom of expression, where everybody is allowed to say what they want, thereby hiding the inequality of the positions of our speech, which first of all makes them political. This is why Blanchot argues that the language of politics favours the dialogue of equality, as it tends to increase the destruction of society (IC 81). Here we fail to realize the fundamental role of language as the irreducible medium of the community in reducing it again to a mere means of the communication of information. To welcome the stranger means to take care of our language and to allow it its particularity. The challenge of literature to politics, then, lies in what Blanchot calls *plural speech*. This is a speech that can never be reduced to one meaning, neither in the ideal sense of signification, nor with respect to the position of a single indemnified subject.

Such a society Blanchot calls a community without communion, and he comes to see such a society more and more in the history of the Jewish people (IC 123–30). We can see through Jewish history that the Jewish community is not as centred around the idea of communion, in which the Christian experiences, for example, the unity of the Church and the faithful, a unity which has often been compared to that of the different parts of a living organism. While it seems to be the idea of religion to give rise to a community of human beings, the lack of communion in the Jewish community, for Blanchot, cannot be seen as a weakness, leading to a dispersion of the Jews into individuality. Rather, there can be a community that does not sustain itself by recourse to an imaginary identity leading to nationalistic doctrine. Such a community sustains itself through an idea of dispersion, of the continuous political demand of going outside of its established ways. It is this idea of dispersion or nomadic life that makes this community ideal. But it is also this that gives rise to persecution. The Jew has always appeared in Europe as the suspect. Not the one who is guilty and thus fits into the juridical system, but the one who escapes the system, whose very existence appears as a constant threat to the system as such: in Judaism we find the 'going outside' as an essential ethical demand. This 'outside' is not to be understood in geographical terms, but as an openness of a tradition that understands itself as being continually disrupted by the movement of writing and history. We have seen above that the human being is constituted like a literary work, and it is in Judaism that Blanchot finds a religion which understands truth as the historical process of the interpretation of the scriptures, in opposition to Christianity which, behind the writing of the Bible, always looks for an unhistorical truth given in the spoken word of Jesus. Judaism hence appears to Blanchot as a way out of the racist and fascist trials of the twentieth century. Here he finds 'a rejection of myths, a forswearing of idols, the recognition of an ethical order mani-festing itself in respect for the law' (BR 221). That is why Blanchot remembers so well the moment when demonstrators in the streets of Paris in May 1968 shouted 'We are all German Jews'. In this slogan he sees manifested the most essential demand of the political: going outside of any identity that becomes established. It is here that Blanchot most decisively distinguishes himself from Heidegger (see esp. Chapters 3 and 4). Against the latter's 'paganism' he posits the more essential experience of Judaism, namely that 'truth is nomadic' (L 189). Such a community never fully integrates itself into the customs of its land; it is never one with itself but sustains this constant demand to uproot itself, to continually disrupt the formation of an overbearing identity of its society.

WHAT IS ENGAGED LITERATURE?

From the beginning of this chapter onwards we have asked ourselves what it means for a community to be solely based on language. If community concerns the relations between human beings without reducing them to an abstract universal idea of a subject, then we need another experience of language, one that does not make us all the same, but of a non-dialectical speech that approaches the truth of the foreigner (IC 63). Such a language cannot be that of political engagement, but rather of an engagement of literature, which has always desired to fight for human freedom within the world (BR 144), rather than serving as a means of cultured distraction.

While literature is said to relate to the outside of the world, insofar as the latter is understood as the totality of reflected human action – we might as well say, as everything that is the case – this outside is not completely separate from the world, but is its limit. Literature is then engaged in bringing us to our own truth as living in a world that does not exhaust the meaning of our existence. Jean-Luc Nancy, a contemporary French philosopher, describes this in the following terms:

> In writing's communication, what does the singular being become? It becomes nothing that it is not already: it becomes its own truth, it becomes simply *the truth*.
>
> (ICN 78)

If we speak about engaged literature, we expect this engagement to be directed at the truth. But how does one engage oneself? In Chapter 2 we mentioned the difference between Blanchot and Sartre in relation to the latter's development of the idea of engaged literature in *What is Literature?* (1947). Blanchot there seemed to oppose the idea of an engaged literature, since it would supply an overarching theory of literature, not in step with its anti-theoretical impetus. We now need to discuss this difference in greater detail. In Sartre's book, literature is portrayed as engaging in the world of action and thereby appears itself as action. Although Sartre also argues that the work of literature rends itself free of the artist and becomes the very act of engagement, it nonetheless seems to posit one political position against others. That is not to say that Sartre understands an engaged work of literature as a pamphlet, trying to persuade the reader to accept a specific political interpretation of human society. Instead he claims that literature, the written word not subdued to direct signification, essentially presents a communication engaged in the freedom of human existence. It is, then, as Sartre claims, impossible to write a racist novel. Any work of literature proposes a certain image of the human being, but the essentially free relation of literature cannot purvey an image of the human as denying freedom to some while granting it to others. Sartre could have read an early essay by Blanchot, 'From Revolution to Literature' (1937), which defends a similar position.

Besides this more general point, there is the particular engagement of a specific work of literature. Every work is engaged, not only those that explicitly take any political 'position'. Rather, a work of literature could not even take such a position, as it lies outside the world of means and ends. But there are obviously those books which pretend not to be involved in any political question, even novels which claim to be no more than a way to pass a few hours of spare time. Yet, as Blanchot argues, those works which present themselves as essentially apolitical, present, even if unwittingly, a meaning of the human being as essentially isolated and individualistic; but such a presentation already implies a whole theory of the human being in its relation to the political sphere, that is, an a-political stance is already a hidden political stance. Such a politics is particularly dangerous, since, pretending not to carry a message, this message presents itself as simply and unquestionably 'true'. Here the work becomes 'the servant of everyone's ideas' (WF 192).

Yet, while the literary work is engaged quite independently from the writer, he or she nevertheless faces a responsibility as a writer or, rather, as an intellectual.

> The intellectual is a portion of ourselves, which not only distracts us momentarily from our task, but returns us to what is going on in the world, in order to judge or appreciate what is going on there.
>
> (BR 207)

The authors of literature find themselves in an ambiguous position. As authors they can only resist the system, without properly being able to take a position. In a characterization of this ambiguity which could well be a description of the suspicion that the Communist Party had always shown with regard to Sartre's engagement in their cause, Blanchot writes:

> It is easy to understand why men who have committed themselves to a party, who have made a decision, distrust writers who share their views; because these writers have also committed themselves to literature, and in the final analysis literature, by its very activity, denies the substance of what it represents. This is its law and its truth.
>
> (WF 309–10)

From here stems Blanchot's constant relation to the bad faith involved in a facile idea of engaged literature. Literature denies the substance of that which it represents, as it is the movement of freedom; but all political movement drives towards the existence of a certain political order. For that reason, to subject literature to politics is an act of bad faith.

The problem that Blanchot has with Sartre's idea of engaged literature is then twofold: it concerns, on the one hand, the idea of activity on the part of the engaged work, while, on the other hand, he criticizes the intellectual in Sartre. The intellectual Sartre gains the force of his influence from the writer Sartre, and in this case he misappropriates this influence by extending it to his own particular choices and moral positions (BR 224), thereby attempting to appropriate his own work. It is in this respect that he is, as regards his own work, in bad faith.

But what then is the responsibility of an author? We know it already: the interruption of the political on the part of the intellectual. Now we are able to understand the whole sentence that we have quoted in part above: 'To write is to engage oneself; but to write is also to disengage oneself, to commit oneself irresponsibly' (WF 26). The danger of literature lies, as we have seen, in that it speaks with an anonymous voice, breaking through the identification of meaning with authority. That is to say that writing is dangerous precisely because it is innocent (F 64), putting in question the institutionalization of power. Here in the 1960s, as much as before in the 1930s, Blanchot's politics remains revolutionary, and it is not until an essay called 'Intellectuals under Scrutiny' (1984; in BR 220–1) that Blanchot criticizes his own revolutionary conception of politics, especially his stance from the 1930s, making his peace with the democratic foundation of our societies.

Such a critique is not a complete negation of his earlier stance, but rather a reinterpretation of it. In other words, to the extent that his critique of our culture remains valid, the idea of literature remains that of revolution. And revolutionary action remains, as he writes in 'Literature and the Right to Death', 'in every aspect analogous to action as embodied in literature' (WF 319). The time of the revolution is then the high time of literature, 'the time during which literature becomes history' (WF 321).

What changes with Blanchot's idea of literature and its engagement is that while the writer still looks for the ability to say the world – that is, to put its truth into words, contributing to human knowledge – it is the indirect way by which literature approaches the world that changes the idea of freedom, community and communication. The clearest expression given by Blanchot in this direction can be found in his outline of the main aims of the *Revue Internationale*:

> The intention of the revue is to try to prepare a new possibility, which would allow the author to *say* the 'world' ... but as an author and in the perspective proper to him, with the responsibility which comes to him from the only truth of the writer: thus a form of responsibility (though no less essential) wholly different from that which has brutally marked the relations of literature and public life since 1945, known to us through the simplistic name of 'Sartrean engagement'. Notably, the result of this is that the revue cannot interest itself directly in political reality, but always in an indirect manner. This search for the 'indirect' is one of the major tasks of the revue ...
>
> (L 185)

Here lies the rift with the Sartrean idea of engaged literature, and it will lead us to a completely different idea of communism.

LITERARY COMMUNISM

We have already invoked Sartre and the similarity between his philosophy and that of Blanchot, a similarity which is explained by both of them writing within and about the same historical situation, namely France before, during and after the Second World War, and we have already seen that they are, in this similarity, diametrically opposed to each other. For Sartre, the human being finds itself in a situation and, from within this situation, makes his or her own existence. For Sartre, in other words, the human being is still the *homo faber*, the one who is the maker of its own fate, even if it has to form its existence not from free will, but from the double recognition of the limitation given through the world and the absoluteness of the other human being.

Mankind is understood as making its own history, thus bringing forth its own essence, and because this essence is given as the relation to others, the human being brings forth its essence in the form of its community. It creates itself by making its history through the political struggle for the organization of human society. We have seen in the last chapter that, for Blanchot, such a formulation of political engagement is fatal, as it aligns itself with the idea of politics as rational management, and is finally destined to reduce the political. For Blanchot the whole desperation of Sartre's move from Marxism to Maoism, that is, to the more radical communist ideas of Chairman Mao Zedong (1893–1976), architect and leader of the Chinese Communist Party, can be explained through his attempt to cling to the idea of a direct and active political stance. Such political engagement attempts to bring about the ideal society even if at the price of the catastrophe of the current one. We have seen that Blanchot thinks of a more indirect engagement and disengagement of the literary work, interrupting the political. And yet, he begins with the famous Sartrean pronouncement to the effect that 'communism is the unsurpassable political horizon of our age'. This is expressed in the sentence we have already quoted: 'I would again take up a reflection, never in fact interrupted ... concerning the communist exigency' (UC 2).

But what is communism in Blanchot's view? And what links the idea of communism essentially to the political ideal of Judaism and the question of literature? Following the unity of the words community, communism, communication, communion, we can see that Blanchot has something more essential in mind than a particular political view. That communism is the unsurpassable horizon of our age, lies first of all in that the question of communism is the question of the possibility of political life itself. That is to say that Blanchot does not see communism as one ideology confronting others. Rather, what it confronts is the liberal conception of the private individual as a negation of the political. Consequently communism, for Blanchot, posits the possibility of the political against its demise in modern, economically driven societies. Political life concerns the communal existence of human beings in freedom, while the existence of a great number of private individuals is at best pitiful. The possibility of the human being can then be summarized as: 'real freedom, the achievement of the human community, reason as principle of unity, in other words, a totality that must be called – in the full sense – communist' (F 107).

It is then quite clear that communism for Blanchot does not signify the idea of a totalitarian regime, which subdues the individual to the state. Quite to the contrary, communism, as the idea of the community as a relation between different human beings, continually puts into question the idea of the community. The question of communism is then the fundamental question of the possibility of community:

> Communism is this as well: the incommensurable communication where every-thing that is public – and then everything is public – ties us to the other (others) through what is closest to us.
>
> (F 149)

Communism, as the relation to the other as other, opposes the fortification and standstill of a political system. This is an interpretation of communism directed against our common understanding of it, and it draws its inspiration mainly from the political writings of Blanchot's personal friend Georges Bataille. Communism is here itself the idea of a weakened permanent revolution. 'Weakened' insofar as it does not subscribe to the idea of a glorious revolution that will bring about the perfect state. Rather, communism is the idea of a political system constantly interrupting the tendency of political institutions towards institutionalization. Communism is thus the idea of the political excluded from any established community, or, as Blanchot argues, following Bataille, in a somewhat dense formulation, it is the community of those who have no community.

The inspiration that communism gains from Judaism concerns the foundation of a political state without recourse to myth; and it is this inspiration that marks the shift in Blanchot's political commitment, insofar as the 1930s had seen a Blanchot demanding the return to the founding myth of a nationalist France. This was the struggle that communism had lost against the fascist movements before the war. Fascism attempted to promise the community of the nation by means of a founding myth that unites a people in a common destiny, the fulfilment of which would bring an authentic existence for all. Instead fascism has been seen to be the most extreme institutionalization of politics, even in places where it has not led to war. On the contrary, communism, for Bataille and Blanchot, is a politics that neither promises a final redemption, nor takes the weight of the political from people's shoulders. This is why Bataille, opposing the view that the individual could find its place in a fulfilled communion, argues that a fulfilled and free existence can only be gained by losing oneself. Here the individual neither disappears in the community nor stands autonomously and heroically outside of it.

It is the experience of literature that gives us a clue as to Blanchot's understanding of communism. We have seen above in what sense the community of literature serves as a model for understanding the political, which now becomes the problem of a community that must continually disrupt itself. Literature, while being the space of the community, does not give rise to a communion. Only where the reductive forces of culture have brought about the ruin of literature is it possible to find a nationalistic pride in belonging to the people of whatever author. In other words, whoever takes pride in being a member of the race that has produced a Shakespeare or a Goethe, at the same time brings about the death of literature. The import of literature, then, is that it is neither nationalistic nor universalistic, but at any moment revolutionary.

For Blanchot, communism, far from being an ideology amongst others, answers to the most difficult task of our time, namely to a transformation of the political.

> It is undoubtedly the task of our age to move toward an affirmation that is entirely *other*. A difficult task, essentially risky. It is to this task that communism recalls us with a rigor that it itself often shirks, and it is also to this task that 'artistic experience' recalls us in the realm that is proper to it. A remarkable coincidence.

(F 97)

On the first page of many of his books you will find the inscription: 'Maurice Blanchot, novelist and critic, was born in 1907. His life is entirely dedicated to literature and the silence that belongs to it.' By now we have seen that this stance is far from a withdrawal from politics into the private life of an author.

SUMMARY

The question of politics, that is, the question of how to achieve the good of any human community, arises in the vicinity of literature, as both litera- ture and politics concern themselves with the human community, which is separate from the world of knowledge and information. The political, as Blanchot constantly reminds us, is not based on the level of administra- tion or economics, but on the ethical community of human beings. Insofar as my relation to the other human being is not one of knowledge, Blanchot argues that it can only be broached by art, especially by literature. Like the political, literature is not concerned with increasing our knowledge of the world, but with the articulation of the community. According to Blanchot, we have to understand language from the position of literature and the relation between human beings from the model of the relation between author and reader. It is from this position that the individual can be understood as structured like a literary work.

To understand Blanchot's approach to engaged literature we have compared it to that of Jean-Paul Sartre. Both share many of their basic premises, especially as to the relation between human beings deter- mining the realm of the political. Against the background of these similarities, the specific approach of Blanchot became clear: for him the other human being who appears suddenly in my world gives rise only to an experience of the inability to master this relation. From here Blanchot turns to an idea of communism as the constant disruption of the political sphere. For Blanchot, communism determines the ideal of a literary community, insofar as it aims at a community without communion, that is, a community in which the individual is not reduced to being a particular instantiation of the universal idea of a citizen.

The main difference between Sartre's idea of engaged literature and Blanchot's 'anti-theory' of literature, then, consists in that the former subjects literature to the political, thereby misunderstanding both. Literature cannot serve political ends because it is always disrupting not only our ideas of the political but also the idea of literature itself. The act of writing, as Blanchot shows, is dangerous insofar as it puts into ques- tion any institutionalization of power, including that of communist states.

Criticizing the Sartrean approach to the idea of engaged literature, Blanchot outlines a novel approach that combines literature, Judaism and communism into the ideal of a literary community. He describes Judaism as a religion free of a mythical foundation, accounting for the literary constitution of human existence. It is this thought that will allow us to escape, on the one hand, the threat of fascism as the dream of a communion based on myth, and, on the other, the threat of a reduction of politics to an idea of governance in the political indifference of liberal democracy.

AFTER BLANCHOT

Having discussed Blanchot's criticism of the idea that a text finds its meaning in the intentions of an author, we have to be as clear as possible that when we speak about Blanchot's influence, we refer to the influence of the books that have appeared in this name. Or, rather, we are thinking about the impact that the work called 'Blanchot' has had on the contemporary scene of literary criticism, philosophy and related subject areas. Speaking of a work here is to say that we are not looking for sentences of his books being quoted in other books by other theorists, but at the impact of the questions and problems posed by his text.

The disappearance of the writer places the work firmly within current critical theory. This is not to say that his work refers to long lines of proper names that go into the distant past and serve as an image of intellectual historical development. It is not that we somehow begin with Plato and end up with Blanchot, who then has other names following after him, so that all these names are chained together like beads on a necklace. Instead Blanchot hardly ever names his references. He is not concerned with intellectual property, neither with his own nor that of other authors. In the end we are not concerned with originality, as if we had understood anything just by realizing that it is an insight 'proper to Blanchot'. We think we have come to grips with a work once we have been able to dissolve it into a line of proper names, that is, once we have identified the provenance of all ideas appearing in it, while it should be quite clear that such an interpretation brings us no closer to the meaning of a work. To dissolve a work into influences is to get rid of the work, to deny it any real influence on one's own conceptions.

This is why, for Blanchot, writing is essentially anonymous, both as to its author and as to the different influences upon it. And, it no more acknowledges its sources than it insists on its influence on other writers. To be placed firmly within our intellectual history is to be indistinguishable, to respond to the task of writing without being concerned about oneself, without using the work to further one's own fame. Blanchot's reticence in naming his sources has nothing to do with laziness or the attempt to claim other ideas as his own. His reticence about appearing in public under the power of his proper name is not merely a personal quirk, but a living out of the demand of writing: the writer must disappear in order that the work may leave its mark.

And yet, at first this disappearance of the writer might appear contradictory once we look at Blanchot's text, inscribed as it is by friendship. Friendship seems to denote a relation not between different works, but between people. Why should we be interested in these friendships if our aim is to understand the work? We know how influential the friendships with Georges Bataille and Emmanuel Levinas were in respect to Blanchot's development. We know as well that one cannot underestimate the impact that Blanchot had on Jacques Derrida and the movement called deconstruction, in which the question of the possibility of literature, the 'death of the author', ethics and justice are important topics. We have even heard that Michel Foucault dreamt of being Maurice Blanchot. What has all this to do with the work? These friendships were not just easy relations of complicity and like-mindedness, but brought both parties face to face with that which exceeds them. To be a friend is to cease to be what one is. It is a relation of estrangement. Only in the eyes of the Other do I exceed my existence as an isolated being. This holds not only for the actuality of friendship, but especially for the exigency of writing. We can, for example, look at the first part of *The Unavowable Community*, a text that has its motivation in a book by Jean-Luc Nancy, itself reflecting on the importance of Bataille's political thought. Now this appears as a clear lineage of influence, but Blanchot does not seem to write directly about either Nancy's or Bataille's work, whilst at the same time not writing about anything else. It is as if these two works first of all allow

Blanchot to forget about his own views or those of anybody else, in order to write the political. In a strange way, then, this question of friendship does not contradict the disappearance of the writer. Rather than bringing her back into the limelight it first of all seems to allow for her disappearance. It is precisely in this relation that one loses the familiarity with one's own work as well as the other's. We can see from here why Blanchot has claimed that the estrangement of writing can serve as the basis of understanding the reality of human relations and therefore the idea of the political:

> Man can become the impossible friend of man, his relation to the latter being
> precisely with the impossible: sufficiency is shattered, communication is no
> longer that of separated beings who promise each other a recognition in the
> infinitely distant future of a world without separation; it is not content with
> bringing together particular individuals in the intimacy of desire; communica-
> tion alone affirms itself, it affirms itself not as a movement that affirms what it
> unites but denies it, the movement itself being without assurance, without
> certainty.
>
> (F 96)

Such uncertainty spoils the idea of separating clearly which thought belongs properly to the work of one thinker or that of another. But we can see that such a description of the mutual penetration of writing fits better into a reality where we were often used to find quite spurious explanations of how a thought could have passed from one author to another where there were obviously no relations between them, so that we were reduced to make use of vague metaphors like 'this idea must have been in the air'.

In fact, we tend to know Blanchot's work in its most anonymous fashion, namely without even being aware of it. That is, in the Anglo-American world, those who read Blanchot usually do not do so first hand, but through the work of others, especially that of Jacques Derrida, whose work stands at the beginning of a revival of literary theory from the 1970s onwards. Indeed, Blanchot is the most impor-tant precursor to what is called deconstruction and it is difficult to find an idea in Derrida's work that is not also present in the writings of Blanchot. Indeed, Blanchot's writings have been decisive with respect to many contemporary French thinkers, including Roland Barthes, Michel Foucault and Gilles Deleuze. While the vast majority of twentieth-century French thought found a common starting point in Kojève's lectures on Hegel, it is particularly Bataille's and Blanchot's interpretation of these that have become the 'French face of Hegelianism'.

Like every writer, Blanchot's work returns again and again to the same theme, and this theme is language. Like Mallarmé, however, he is not a linguist. His aim is not to produce a new theory within the science of language, as we might find such a theory, for example, in the work of the American linguist Noam Chomsky (1928–), but to describe language from the perspective of literature. In so doing, he is attempting to bring some of our traditional conceptions of language into question. Thus we have seen that language, if one begins with literature, is no longer understood as the expression of our thoughts. In traditional linguistics, on the contrary, the study of language begins with the speaking subject. The metaphysical status of such a subject is left unthought, precisely because it allows us to make of language an object of scientific investigation. This stance becomes questionable once we realize that language appears on a more fundamental level, so as to make it impossible to reduce it to a specific function. From the side of literature, as we have seen, language is not felt as the speaking of someone, it is not experienced as a translation of intentional thought, but appears from out of the anonymous source of the 'one speaks'. One must understand that this experience of language is not simply an addition to the positive description of language, but calls into question the status of the subject as origin of language. This re-conceptualization of language, most importantly in the works of Hegel, Nietzsche, Heidegger and Blanchot, has decisively changed the landscape of European thought, in all its different areas, from linguistics, metaphysics, ethics and politics to aesthetics and, especially, literary theory. These philosophies attempt to come to grips with what Nietzsche has called 'the death of God', as it leads to the fragmentation of our experience. Blanchot has then inherited a question, on which he elaborates throughout the whole of his work, namely that of the finitude of our existence, expressing itself in a new, disturbing and seemingly meaningless experience of death. Here it is no longer the powerful subject that gives meaning to its world, but a passive human being that listens to the anonymous voice of the other.

This means that the question of literature, in which at least for Blanchot this anonymity has its greatest force, is no longer a parochial question about values and taste, but directly a philosophical question about the status of the human being, and that this question itself has a broader ethical and political significance. Literary language as the displacement of the subject seems to us to be the kernel of what would later be called deconstruction. The latter is not merely a method of critical analysis that examines certain assumptions present in a text, but a philosophical project that engages in a thoroughgoing interrogation of the metaphysics of the subject. The question of literature was and always has been more for Derrida then merely an aesthetic one, that is, more than a question for a subjective feeling or the value of certain works of art. Insofar as this method does consist of close analyses of texts this always happens with respect to the general philosophical questions that Blanchot himself had already raised.

This leads us finally to one last effect of Blanchot's writings on the French cultural scene, and, consequently, on Anglo-American literary theory. As soon as the question of literature ceases to be reduced to the question of the meaning of texts, it breaks out of its enclosure within any one particular genre. The literary work can no longer be reduced to being 'a novel' or 'a narrative', nor can the study of literature strictly be distinguished, for example, from history, sociology or philosophy. Literature itself, as a separate self-enclosed academic subject is a recent invention, but one that is already vanishing, not least under the influence of Blanchot's work. This does not mean that we will no longer ask questions about literature, but the straitjacket of 'literary studies' will have been broken. This is the greatest impact of Blanchot's writings: to think about literature, to struggle with the question of literature, is to face the most fundamental questions of our age.

FURTHER READING

This section includes both works by Maurice Blanchot himself and secondary material on Blanchot.

WORKS BY MAURICE BLANCHOT

1 *Thomas the Obscure, New Version*, trans. Robert Lamberton (D. Lewis, New York, 1973).

Originally published in France in 1941 (Blanchot withdrew the first version). How to summarize a book whose main concern lies not so much with the events happening to its protagonist called Thomas, but with its style? Written in the most lucid prose, it constantly slides into meaninglessness. In terms of Blanchot's literary criticism it is highly important for his meditations on the impossibility of death. It acts as a literary counterpoint to the more formal analyses of death in the essay 'Literature and the Right to Death' and in parts of *The Space of Literature*. This work is also to be found in the *Station Hill Blanchot Reader* (see below).

2 *Death Sentence*, trans. Lydia Davis (Station Hill Press, Barrytown, NY, 1978).

This is an astonishingly original novel that is ostensibly set in Paris at the beginning of the Second World War. It is the story of the relation between the narrator and two women, one of whom appears to be terminally ill. Like *Thomas the Obscure*, it is not the narrative that is important, but the atmosphere of the book. From a purely theoretical side, one can make connections to the themes of death and dying, and the excessive demand of writing that appears in Blanchot's literary criticism. This work is also to be found in the anthology *The Station Hill Blanchot Reader* (see below).

3 *The Gaze of Orpheus, and Other Literary Essays*, ed. P. Adams Sitney, trans. Lydia Davis (Station Hill Press, Barrytown, NY, 1981).

This is one of the first collections of Blanchot's work in English, which is now out of print, and most of the essays can be found in the *Station Hill Blanchot Reader* (see below).

4 *The Madness of the Day*, trans. Lydia Davis (Station Hill Press, Barrytown, NY, 1981).

This is one of Blanchot's short narratives and was originally published in French in 1973. Like all of Blanchot's narratives, the story tells us little. Ostensibly, it seems to be about someone who has been incarcerated in a mental hospital, but knowing that tells you almost nothing, and the text resists interpretation, even though its very opacity and enigmatic nature seems to invite it.

5 *The Sirens' Song, Selected Essays,* ed. G. Josipovici, trans. S. Rabinovitch (The Harvester Press, Brighton, 1982).

This collection is one of first selections of Blanchot's work in English and it is no longer in print. It has a fine introductory essay by the editor Gabriel Josipovici. Most of the essays are now translated elsewhere in the complete translations of Blanchot's work such as *The Space of Literature* and *The Work of Fire* (see below).

6 *The Space of Literature*, trans. A. Smock (University of Nebraska Press, Lincoln and London, 1982).

Perhaps this book, first published in France in 1955, is the most important and influential of Blanchot's works. In this book he examines the process of reading as well as artistic creativity. Central to this work, also, is Blanchot's most sustained inquiry into the relation between literature and death, 'The Work and the Space of Death'. Key writers that are discussed in this book are Stéphane Mallarmé, Franz Kafka and Rainer Maria Rilke.

7 *The Step not Beyond*, trans. L. Nelson (State University of New York Press, Albany, 1982).

This is Blanchot's first book that is written in the fragmentary style (the next will be *The Writing of Disaster*, see below). The important themes of this work are writing, death and the neuter and the key writers are G.W.F. Hegel and Friedrich Nietzsche, rather than the literary figures that predominate elsewhere in Blanchot's work.

8 *Vicious Circles, Two Fictions and 'After the Fact'*, trans. P. Auster (Station Hill Press, Barrytown, NY, 1985).

This collection is a translation of two narratives by Blanchot, 'The Idyll' and 'The Last Word', and also a post-face called 'After the Fact'. The first two stories can be found in the *Station Hill Blanchot Reader* (see below).

9 *The Writing of Disaster*, trans. A. Smock (University of Nebraska Press, Lincoln and London, 1986).

After *The Space of Literature*, this book is perhaps the most influential of Blanchot's works. It is written in the same fragmentary style as *The Step not Beyond*, but its themes are even wider and it is difficult to typify it either as a literary or philosophical work. Its central theme is perhaps all the disasters that have befallen human beings in the twentieth century, all of which are represented for Blanchot by the impossible image of the death camps like Auschwitz. It also contains important fragments on the philosophy of Emmanuel Levinas, continuing his engagement with this work in *The Infinite Conversation*.

10 *The Unavowable Community*, trans. P. Joris (Station Hill Press, Barrytown, NY, 1988).

This book, which is one of Blanchot's most recent, is a meditation on the possibility of community in modern times. It is also an explicit response to Jean-Luc Nancy's *The Unworkable Community*. It consists of two parts, first a reflection on the political thought of his friend Georges Bataille, then an essay on the political significance of the novels of Marguerite Duras.

11 *The Infinite Conversation*, trans. S. Hanson (University of Minnesota Press, Minneapolis and London, 1993).

The largest of Blanchot's books by far, containing a very wide range of material including essays on Franz Kafka, Blaise Pascal, Friedrich Nietzsche, Bertolt Brecht and Albert Camus. It also contains Blanchot's fullest engagement with Levinas's ethics. The important themes of this work are the nature of language, the narrative voice, revolutionary politics, the meaning and scope of nihilism, and Jewish identity. It is also in this work that the division between Blanchot's critical and literary work becomes blurred, an experiment in style that will be furthered in *The Step not Beyond* and *The Writing of Disaster* (see above).

12 *The Work of Fire*, trans. C. Mandell (Stanford University Press, Stanford, 1995).

This work is a translation of some of Blanchot's earliest essays, which were originally published in this form in 1949, and it contains one of the most important essays of Blanchot's work, 'Literature and the Right to Death'. This early essay holds the kernel of his approach to the question of literature and would be one of the best places to start reading his work. There are also significant essays here on Stéphane Mallarmé and Franz Kafka.

13 *The Blanchot Reader*, ed. M. Holland (Blackwell, Oxford, 1995).

An interesting collection of Blanchot's work that is not available in other editions. It is especially useful in that it contains some translations of Blanchot's political writings. It does not contain, however, some of the more important of Blanchot's writings, and has perhaps been superseded by the *Station Hill Blanchot Reader* (see below).

14 *The Most High*, trans. Allan Stoekl (University of Nebraska Press, Lincoln, 1996).

One of Blanchot's earliest novels whose style has much in common with the work of Franz Kafka. The ostensible plot of this novel is the destruction of a city through a mysterious disease, but it is also a profound meditation on the power of the state and human weakness and frailty.

15 *Friendship*, trans. E. Rottenberg (Stanford University Press, Stanford, 1997).

This is the last of Blanchot's standard critical works that consist of literary reviews and was originally published in 1971. Like these other works it contains essays on writers and works of literature, but perhaps differently from these it takes on both a more autobiographical flavour, for example, in the testimony to his friendship with Georges Bataille (from which this collection takes its title), and also a more directly political stance with essays on Karl Marx, some of which were the result of his engagement in the student riots in Paris in 1968.

16 *Awaiting Oblivion*, trans. John Gregg (University of Nebraska Press, Lincoln, 1997)

One of Blanchot's late fictions that begins to move away from the traditional idea of a novel or a short story and which Blanchot called 'narratives'. In style this is close to the work of Samuel Beckett. What is significant is not what 'happens', which on the surface appears to be a conversation between a man and a woman set, like many of

Blanchot's later narratives, in an anonymous hotel room, but its unravelling through fragmentary writing.

17 *The Station Hill Blanchot Reader*, ed. G. Quasha, trans. P. Auster, L. Davis and R. Lamberton (Station Hill Press, Barrytown, NY, 1998).

This is an excellent anthology of Blanchot's writing that contains both the finest examples of his narrative writing, such as *Thomas the Obscure*, *Death Sentence* and *Madness of the Day*, and also eleven essays that were originally published in *The Gaze of Orpheus*. Some of these essays are among the most important that Blanchot wrote, such as 'Literature and the Right to Death' and 'The Narrative Voice'. This anthology is also a testimony to the commitment of the Station Hill Press to the work of Blanchot and the important work of their translators, some of whom are significant writers in their own right, such as Paul Auster and Lydia Davies.

WORKS ON MAURICE BLANCHOT

1 Bruns, Gerald L., *Maurice Blanchot: The Refusal of Philosophy* (Johns Hopkins University Press, Baltimore, 1997).

A detailed and sophisticated interpretation of the philosophical and political background of Blanchot's writing that covers the whole period of his work. It especially concentrates on the relation of his work to the poetics of Heidegger and offers a stimulating comparison to the poet Paul Celan.

2 Clark, Timothy, *Derrida, Heidegger, Blanchot: Sources of Derrida's Notion and Practice of Literature* (Cambridge University Press, Cambridge, 1992).

A very readable and scholarly book and one of the first studies in English to demonstrate the importance of Blanchot for understanding contemporary literary theory. It shows the thread of influence from Heidegger via Blanchot to Derrida's notions of literature.

3 Critchley, Simon, *Very Little – Almost Nothing* (Routledge, London and New York, 1997).

Although not a book directly about Blanchot it is deeply inspired by his writings. Its first part offers an insightful and wide-ranging interpretation of the 'there is' that encompasses the alliance between literature and death, and of Blanchot's relation to Emmanuel Levinas. One of its most interesting parts is the reading of Samuel Beckett, which in a certain sense puts Blanchot's anti-theory of literature into practice.

4 Deleuze, Gilles, *Foucault*, trans. S. Hand (University of Minnesota Press, Minneapolis, 1988).

Although this is not a book about Blanchot but Foucault, his name figures in it quite prominently. Deleuze is clear that the origin of Foucault's understanding of language, which is central to his critical project, is to be found in Blanchot's work. It is also certain from reading Deleuze's comments how important Blanchot was to his own distancing from modern semiology. One of the key books for demonstrating the importance of Blanchot to the French radical thinkers of the last decades.

5 Gill, Carolyn Bailey, ed., *Maurice Blanchot: The Demand of Writing* (Routledge, New York and London, 1996).

A collection of fourteen critical essays which cover most of the different aspects of Blanchot's work, such as his politics, his narratives and his literary criticism. Some of the essays are explanatory, whereas others critically engage with Blanchot's work. It also contains a letter from Blanchot in which he addresses the contentious issue of his political involvement in the 1930s.

6 Gregg, John, *Maurice Blanchot and the Literature of Transgression* (Princeton University Press, Princeton, 1994).

This is a challenging book that requires a long familiarity with Blanchot's work. It is organized around the concept of transgression that, Gregg argues, Blanchot took over from Georges Bataille. Other topics are Blanchot's critique of Hegel, his description of the relation between literature and death, and his use of biblical figures in the depiction of reading and writing. The second part of the book involves a very detailed reading of two of Blanchot's works of fiction: *The Most High* and *Awaiting Oblivion*.

7 Hill, Leslie, *Blanchot: Extreme Contemporary* (Routledge, London and New York, 1997).

A demanding introduction, which is by far the most useful work in English on Blanchot. It gives a very good biography of Blanchot at the beginning and does much to dispel some of the myths surrounding his journalism of the 1930s. It also covers the broad sweep of Blanchot's literary criticism from the 1940s to recent times. This is not the easiest work and requires some philosophical knowledge, but it will deepen the reader's understanding of Blanchot.

8 Libertson, Joseph, *Proximity: Levinas, Blanchot, Bataille, and Communication* (Martinus Nijhoff, The Hague, 1982).

One of the first books in English on the work of Blanchot. It is a fascinating study because it attempts to link Blanchot's work with Levinas and Bataille. It is, however, written in the most forbidding academic style, which makes its difficult to read. Not for the novice.

9 Mehlman, Jeffrey, *Legacies of Anti-Semitism in France* (University of Minnesota Press, Minneapolis, 1983).

Contains the first essay in English that draws attention to Blanchot's political writings of the 1930s. Mehlman puts forward the controversial theory that Blanchot's journalism of this period cannot be totally divorced from French anti-Semitism and nor can his own literary criticism. Worth reading to find out if the other critics are right to dismiss this thesis.

10 Pepper, Thomas, ed., *Yale French Studies: The Places of Maurice Blanchot* (Yale University Press, New Haven, 1998).

A collection of recent essays that unfortunately varies in quality and suffers from the 'lack of distance from Blanchot's style. Their focal point tends to be Blanchot's novels and narratives, rather than his literary criticism. Not really useful as a way into his work, but there are one or two interesting essays to be found in it.

11 Unger, Steven, *Scandal and Aftereffect: Blanchot and France Since 1930* (University of Minnesota Press, Minneapolis, 1995).

A rather specialized book on Blanchot. Again its topic is Blanchot's political writing of the 1930s, which seems to be an obsession of American literary critics. Central to his argument is the psychoanalytic concept of 'aftereffect' that is used to explain the amnesia concerning Blanchot's political involvement. Useful to discover some of the detail of Blanchot's journalism, since most of it remains untranslated.

12 Wall, Thomas Carl, *Radical Passivity: Levinas, Blanchot and Agamben* (State University of New York Press, Albany, 1999).

An exceptional book written in a highly engaging and approachable style. This is not an introductory work, nor entirely a monograph, but an original piece of philosophy in its own right. It focuses on the place of death in Blanchot, but also interestingly links his work to Levinas (and the differences there might be between them) and to the lesser-known Italian philosopher Giorgio Agamben.

INTERNET RESOURCES

1 Lilly, Reginald, *The Resource Page for Readers of Blanchot*. http://
lists.village.virginia.edu/~spoons/blanchot/blanchot_mainpage.htm
(6 March 2000).

An excellent resource for anyone who is interested in Blanchot.
Contains a bibliography of Blanchot's writings and secondary literature
on them in French, English, Italian, Spanish and German. It also offers
links to other Blanchot sites on the Internet and an email discussion list
on Blanchot.

INDEX